The Global and the National

CRITICAL MEDIA STUDIES
INSTITUTIONS, POLITICS, AND CULTURE

Series Editor
Andrew Calabrese, University of Colorado

Recent Titles in the Series
Deliberation, Democracy, and the Media,
   edited by Simone Chambers and Anne Costain
Deregulating Telecommunications: U.S. and Canadian Telecommunications, 1840–1997,
   Kevin G. Wilson
Floating Lives: The Media and Asian Diasporas,
   edited by Stuart Cunningham and John Sinclair
Continental Order? Integrating North America for Cybercapitalism,
   edited by Vincent Mosco and Dan Schiller
Social Theories of the Press: Constituents of Communication Research, 1840s to 1920s,
   second edition, Hanno Hardt
The Global and the National: Media and Communications in Post-Communist Russia,
   Terhi Rantanen
Privacy and the Information Age,
   Serge Gutwirth
Global Media Governance: A Beginner's Guide,
   Seán Ó Siochrú and W. Bruce Girard

Forthcoming in the Series
From Newspaper Guild to Multimedia Union: A Study in Labor Convergence,
   Catherine McKercher
The Eclipse of Freedom: From the Principle of Publicity to the Freedom of the Press,
   Slavko Splichal
Elusive Autonomy: Brazilian Communications Policy in an Age of Globalization and Technical Change, Sergio Euclides de Souza
Internet Governance in Transition,
   Daniel J. Paré
Herbert Schiller,
   Richard Maxwell
Digital Disability: The Social Construction of Disability in New Media,
   Gerard Goggin and Christopher Newell
The Party System and Public Service Broadcasting in Italy,
   Cinzia Padovani

The Global and the National

Media and Communications in Post-Communist Russia

Terhi Rantanen

ROWMAN & LITTLEFIELD PUBLISHERS, INC.
Lanham • Boulder • New York • Oxford

ROWMAN & LITTLEFIELD PUBLISHERS, INC.

Published in the United States of America
by Rowman & Littlefield Publishers, Inc.
An Imprint of the Rowman & Littlefield Publishing Group
4720 Boston Way, Lanham, Maryland 20706
www.rowmanlittlefield.com

12 Hid's Copse Road, Cumnor Hill, Oxford OX2 9JJ, England

Chapter 3 of this volume was previously published as "The Old and the New: Communications Technology and Globalization in Russia," *New Media and Society* 3 (2), 2001 and is used by permission of Sage Publications Ltd.

British Library Cataloguing in Publication Information Available

Library of Congress Cataloging-in-Publication Data
Rantanen, Terhi.
    The global and the national : media and communications in
post-Communist Russia / Terhi Rantanen.
        p.   cm. — (Critical media studies)
    Includes bibliographical references and index.
    ISBN 0-7425-1567-2 (alk. paper)—ISBN 0-7425-1568-0 (pbk. : alk. paper)
    1. Mass media—Russia (Federation)   2. Communication—Russia
(Federation)   I. Title.   II. Series.
    P92.R9 R36   2002
    302.23'0947—dc21   2002001198

Printed in the United States of America

∞ ™ The paper used in this publication meets the minimum requirements of American National Standard for Information Sciences—Permanence of Paper for Printed Library Materials, ANSI/NISO Z39.48-1992.

Contents

Acknowledgments

This book began (although I did not then know it) in 1982 when I went to the Soviet Union for two months to research Soviet news agencies. I was met at a Moscow railway station by Elena Vartanova, then a Ph.D. student, now a professor in the Faculty of Journalism at Moscow State University. It was the beginning of several joint research projects, and a friendship that has lasted for twenty years. Her professional help has been invaluable as has been Professor Yassen Zassoursky's, then and now dean of the Faculty of Journalism at Moscow State University. More recently, I have enjoyed intellectually stimulating discussions with a member of his family, and another member of the faculty, Ivan Zassoursky.

Without the contribution of Dr. Farrell Burnett, this book would look very different. Her literary and scholarly skills helped me to polish my language and improve my argumentation. I am also indebted to Luke Collins, Svetlana Koleshnikova, Ellen Mickiewicz, Jukka Pietiläinen, Andrei Richter, Gwendolyn Sasse, Marsha Siefert, and Stefaan Verhulst for their help.

Some things can be difficult even in the age of globalization: this time it was getting updated data and transferring it across borders. My thanks to Olga Oslin, Timur Nurpeissov, and Maria Suchkova who helped me accomplish this. Shani Orgad, Kris Roger, Cornel Sandvoss and Peter Wren at the London School of Economics and Political Science created the tables I have used and Jim Ottaway indexed the book.

I am also grateful to the Finnish Academy of Sciences, Helsinki University, Moscow State University, the University of Westminster, Wolfson College of University of Oxford, and the London School of Economics and Political Science for providing me with the intellectual, institutional, or financial support that have made my work possible. Last but not least, I am indebted to Andrew Calabrese, Brenda Hadenfeldt, Renee Jardine, Alden Perkins, and Colin Sparks for their help in making a manuscript into a book.

Some of the chapters in this volume have already appeared elsewhere in a different form: chapter 3 was previously published as "The Old and the New: Communications Technology and Globalization in Russia," *New Media and Society* 3 (2), 2001; chapter 4 was previously published as "The Old Meets the New: News agencies in Post-Communist Russia," in *Russian Reports: Studies in Post-Communist Transformation of Media and Journalism*, edited by Jan Ekecrantz and Kerstin Olofsson. Stockholm: Almqvist & Wicksell, 2000; chapter 5 was previously published as "From Export to Import: Russian Television in the Age of Globalization," in *Media, Communications, and the Open Society*, edited by Yassen N. Zassoursky and Elena Vartanova. Moscow: Faculty of Journalism, IKAR Publisher, 1999.

This book is dedicated to Richard, not only for sentimental reasons, but also to tell him something about a country he has never been to.

1

Media and Globalization: Theories and Concepts

There is no globalization without media and communications. Scholars make frequent passing reference to media and communication in globalization, but seldom detail their precise role in it. Instead, their role is often reduced to a merely technological one that thus becomes self-evident, but often is overlooked. Furthermore, most academic studies of globalization concentrate on Western Europe and the United States. But globalization does not only concern the West. Why is it then that globalization theorists make only passing remarks about Russia and then move on to discuss Western Europe or the United States? For as *The Economist* ("A Bad Time to Be an Ostrich," 1998) suggests, a principal cause of globalization is the collapse of Communism. There seems to be a mental iron curtain that prevents writers from acknowledging the importance of Russia as the major post-Communist country that has encountered globalization. More explicitly, in the framework of this book, what is the role of *national media* and communications in the globalization of post-Communist Russia, where the Iron Curtain and, in effect, a *media curtain* limited its citizens' exposure to the global network society for more than six decades? The globalization debate has so far neglected Russia, and perhaps for good reason, considering the evidence from the former superpower, post-Communist Russia—a nation that cannot be unproblematically classified as an advanced first-world country, or an underdeveloped third-world country, or a newly

1

developing country. Roland Robertson foresaw, as early as in 1990, the following:

> Theorizing the topic of globalization is a task that has been made all the more difficult by the recent and continuing events in China, the USSR and Europe which have disrupted virtually all of the conventional views concerning the world order. At the same time those events and the circumstances, which they have created, make the analytical effort all the more urgent. We have entered a phase of what appears to us in 1990 [to be] a great global uncertainty—so much so that the very idea of uncertainty promises to become globally institutionalized. (1990, 16)

Despite Robertson's remarks about the significance of the collapse of Communism for our understanding of globalization, the latter is often described as an individual, universal experience. As John Tomlinson observes, globalization is defined as experience, thus shifting the focus from institutions to individuals (1994, 149). Anthony Giddens writes that globalization is concerned with the "intersection of presence and absence, the interlacing of social events and social relationships 'at distance' with local contextualities" (1991, 21).

Malcolm Waters also emphasizes the experience of globalization by defining it as "a social process in which the constraints of geography on social and cultural arrangements recede and in which people become increasingly aware that they are receding" (1995, 3). It is easy to point to the role that media and communication technology plays in breaking down people's experience of time and space.

Another approach, which emphasizes the universal experience of globalization and has a different starting point, is to evaluate the role of media institutions. In contrast to individuals' experience, media and communication scholars themselves have concentrated mainly on the role of media institutions in the process of globalization (see, for example, Golding and Harris 1997; Herman and McChesney 1997; Boyd-Barrett and Rantanen 1998; Thussu 1998). This is a different level of analysis, which emphasizes communications structures rather than individual experience. Jan Ekecranz lists different aspects of the media and globalization syndrome (1998), among which are:

- communications empires play a significant role in world politics;
- there is an interdependent transnationalization of popular culture and industry;

- post–Cold War structures are evolving fast with increasingly diluted borders between politics and commerce;
- technological imperatives are matched (and often driven by) commercial imperative;
- there is a horizontal integration of communication industries;
- there is a technological convergence between the different sections of communications industries.

This approach contrasts starkly with that which views globalization as individual experience, which is in itself a universal phenomenon. Nevertheless, the two approaches are not mutually exclusive, because the production of media and the experience of them are linked, often in highly subtle ways. National media and communications systems, themselves increasingly subject to globalization, are intermediaries between production and experience. This is an important theme for the purpose of this book: post-Communist Russia is building new national infrastructures within the larger world context of the globalization of media and communications.

Hence, it is impossible to separate the national and the global from each other. However, the consequences of the globalizing processes are not easy to predict. According to James Lull, "globalization is best considered a complex set of interacting and often countervailing human, material, and symbolic flows that lead to diverse, heterogeneous cultural positionings and practices which persistently and variously modify established sectors of social, political and cultural power" (1995, 150). In post-Communist Russia, the concept of globalization needs to be redefined, so that it encompasses the nationalization of global media as well as the globalization of national media. This is the rearticulation of the relationship between the national and the global—the natio-globalization of Russian media.

The globalization of nation states is at the center of the political debate regarding the possible consequences of globalization. There are two schools of globalization theorists who take different positions on the role of nation-states (Gray 1998). Globalization optimists (see, for example, Ohmae 1995) consider national governments as municipalities of the global system—their economies are no longer "national" in any significant sense but they can be effective as governments if they accept their reduced role of providing the local public services that the global economy requires (Hirst and Thompson

1996, 185). In contrast, globalization pessimists see the nation-state as a strong fortress against globalization. Paul Hirst and Graham Thompson observe that the strength of the (nation-) state is its sovereignty—the state being the primary source of binding laws within a given territory (1996, 192).

Neither globalization optimists nor globalization pessimists have taken fully into account the role of media and communications in the process of globalization. This neglect of the role of media and communications has led to a theoretical either/or situation, which misses an essential feature of globalization—the relationship between the global and the national. If scholars outside media and communication research had paid attention to the role of the media, they would have found that media and communication researchers followed similar argumentation. In the media debate, the question was also posed as an either/or choice in which "foreign" was equated with cultural imperialism, and thus threatening to local cultures, while "domestic" was something worth protecting. Only within the theoretical work on globalization has the process been acknowledged as interplay between the global and the national.

As Mike Featherstone observes, "the walls which separate nation-states are increasingly becoming regarded as *permeable* [emphasis mine] as a consequence of some of the trans-societal and global processes" (1995, 82). When he further writes about "the sense of global compression in which the world is increasingly regarded as 'one place' and it becomes much more difficult for nation-states to opt out, avoid the consequences of being drawn together into a progressively tighter figuration through the increasing volume and rapidity of the flows of money, goods, people, information, technology and images" (1995, 81), Featherstone touches upon the issue of media and communications. Again, media and communications are seen as playing a significant role in changing the relationship between global and national—bringing globalization into a national context with the subtlety that only media and communications can achieve. It is not a question of either globalization or nation-states, but a question of the global becoming present in nation-states. In the case of Russia, national media structures are encountering globalization, but this process is being further shaped by strong national forces. Media and communications in post-Communist Russia thus offer an illuminating example of the intersection of the global and the national. The common processes of new media formations—currently taking place all around the world—do not necessarily take similar forms. A country such as post-Communist Russia, where there was a relatively advanced media system that is now in transition, offers scholars a unique glimpse of the multifaceted phenomenon of the intersection of the global and the national.

There are further reasons why research at the level of the nation-state is important. Robertson rightly emphasizes that the prevalence of national societies in the twentieth century is an aspect of globalization. He writes:

> The homogenous nation state—homogenous here in the sense of culturally homogenized, administered citizenry—is thus a construction of a particular form of life. That we ourselves have been increasingly subject to its constraints does not mean that for analytical purposes it has to be accepted as *the* departure point for analyzing and understanding the world. Thus I have argued not merely that national societies should be regarded as constituting *but one* general reference point for the analysis of the global-human circumstance but that we have to recognize even more that we do know that the prevalence of the national society in the twentieth century is an aspect of globalization—that the diffusion of the idea of the national society as a form of institutionalized societalism was central to the accelerated globalization which began to occur over one hundred years ago. (1990, 25–26)

Robertson's argument makes sense in the post-Soviet Russian context even in the twenty-first century. The Soviet Union was a closed and thus homogenous (at least on the surface) society before the collapse of Communism. Elements that are not necessarily present in other countries exist in post-Communist Russia. Russia not only moved from a communist to a capitalist system (as did the other Central and Eastern European countries), but also went from a superpower status to that of a former superpower. It also moved from the union of fifteen Soviet republics to a Russian Federation. The Soviet Union of 286.7 million people became the Russian Federation of 147.7 million people. In addition, the disintegration of the USSR created a Russian diaspora consisting of twenty-five to thirty million people living in newly independent states (Melvin 1995, 5). This is a country that had to reinvent itself politically, economically, and culturally; at the same time, Russia exposed itself to globalization after decades of isolation. "I grew up in a super power, I now live in a third-world country," said a Russian woman when she was asked to describe how she feels about the changes taking place in her native country (Thornhill 1998). Who am I? is the question many Russians frequently ask themselves when almost everything—geography, political identity, nationality and often even the names of places—has changed (Kon 1996, 194).

The mental transition from the Soviet Union to the Russian Federation has been protracted. Most Russians have lived most of their lives in the Soviet Union, under the Communist system, in which Russia accounted for about three-quarters of the USSR's territory and more than half of its population. When Russians were asked how they defined their homeland five years after the USSR had dissolved, for the largest single group (28 percent) it was still the Soviet Union; the next largest group (27 percent) thought it was Russia; nearly as many (25 percent) thought of the region in which they lived, or in which they had grown up (another 17 percent). A large majority (71 percent) thought it was a great misfortune that the Soviet Union no longer existed; and even more (76 percent) thought Russia should unite with its largest neighbor (Kelly et al. 1998, 392). Researchers have also noted a wounded national self-awareness among Russian youth, and chauvinistic moods becoming stronger (Riordan et al. 1995, 22).

One of the key points in the globalization debate has been the declining hold of the nation-state on individuals' identities. As Martin Albrow notes, the state has to accept the competing and crosscutting allegiances of its citizens, up to and even including the point where they are committed to other states (1996, 151). This process is especially pertinent in post-Communist Russia where the state is trying to establish new national identity on the ruins of a former multicultural empire. Several authors have referred to postcommunist countries and their identity in crises (Woodward 1997, 17) or, to use Ernesto Laclau's term, to dislocation of identities (1990, 40). As Jorge Larrain has observed, the question of cultural identity does not usually arise in situations of relative isolation, prosperity and stability (1994, 143). He writes: "For identity to become an issue, a period of instability and crisis, a threat to the old-established ways, is required, especially if this happens in the presence of, or in relation to, other cultural formations." Russia seems to fulfill all these criteria—as long as the Soviet Union was isolated, not wealthy but stable, Soviet identity was not in crisis. After Communism collapsed, there was no Communist or superpower ideology, only the ruins of both. Kelly et al. writes that identities have become of concern not only to individual Russian citizens who are confused about their place in the world, and in their country, after the end of the Soviet rule, but also to the Russian government, to parties and movements, and to political elites (1998, 393–394).

Globalization also challenges the process of national identity-building by producing competing identities. As Manuel Castells puts it, "our world(s), and our lives, are being shaped by the conflicting trends of globalization and identities." He distinguishes three different forms and origins of identity-building that are taking place at the same time: legitimizing, resistance, and project identities (1997, 1, 7–8). Although Castells does not refer to national identities directly, his concept of legitimizing identity comes close to national identity. Castells believes that the dominant institutions of society introduce legitimizing identity, while resistance and project identities are individual responses to the first. He claims that the sources of legitimizing identities are being drained away as a result of the processes of globalization. In post-Communist Russia, however, a civil society—with institutions such as churches, parties, or trade unions—is being created as the country is exposed to globalization. Legitimizing identity in post-Communist Russia is emerging together with other forms of identities. The problem of an emerging legitimizing identity makes post-Communist Russia vulnerable compared to other societies facing globalization and produces resistance identities, especially in the form of nationalism.

As Svetlana Boym observes, it is not accidental that in most post-communist countries today nationalism takes the place of Communist ideology (1994, 287). She writes:

> The seduction of nationalism is the seduction of homecoming and total acceptance: one doesn't even have to join the party; one simply belongs. Nationalist ideology mobilizes the nostalgia for the old commonplace lost and individual nostalgias and family histories, and it also proposes a plan of action for the purification and rebuilding of the collective home. It offers a comforting collective biography instead of a flawed individual story full of estrangements and disappointments;

it promises to recover the blissful childhood of a nation, without the alienation and loss experienced in adult years.

Several writers, the best known of which are Ernest Gellner (1983) and Benedict Anderson (1983), note the role of mass media in establishing and maintaining nationalism. Anderson talks about newspapers and their role in uniting citizens of the same country, most of them never meeting each other, through the ritual of reading newspapers and thus forming imagined communities. As Michael Billig points out, "The nation is to be imagined as a unique entity in terms of time and space. It is imagined as a community stretching through time, with its own past and future destiny: it is imagined across space, embracing the inhabitants of a particular territory" (1995, 70). The notion of imagined community is important for post-Communist Russia in three different ways. First, nation-states may have physical borders that change, as did Russia's when the Soviet Union became the Russian Federation. Second, the Russian past had to be reinvented because both the West and the Russian people have declared over sixty years of the history of the Soviet Union "incorrect." Third, because of the sheer size of most nation-states, the maintenance of nationhood is mediated by different institutions—among them, as Anderson points out, is the press.

Post-Soviet media does not only contribute to the maintenance of nationhood, but also contributes to its creation. It is obvious, as Anderson remarks, that most citizens of the same country never actually meet each other, and thus need the press to share the collective experience of belonging to the same nation. Billig uses the term "flagging" (1995, 8) to describe how established nations remind their citizens of nationhood. The media are among these flagging institutions that contribute to mediated national experiences. The press may have played a major role in creating imagined communities in the past, but has since lost its dominant position to new electronic media. Broadcasting is also seen as contributing to nationalism, although both Gellner and Anderson referred only to printed media (Scannell 1989; Price 1993, 13). In post-Communist Russia there has been a shift from print to electronic culture, and this shift has undeniably contributed to globalization; it also draws our attention mainly to electronic media.

However, to see different media technologies as promoting either globalization or nationalism is an oversimplification. Arjun Appadurai, for example, makes a distinction between the capitalism of the printed word, which territorialized linguistic and cultural communities and consolidated the nation-state, and the electronic capitalism of audiovisual and telecomputerization that are promoting transnational cultural communities (1996, 8). In the case of post-Communist Russia, the media, which are subject to the process of globalization, are also important agents of nationhood—a new nationhood that is being constituted after the collapse of the Soviet Union. When acknowledging the media's dual function, it is not technology (whether electronic or print) that becomes a decisive factor. Media and communications in post-Communist Russia contribute to both globalization and nationalism, and it is the new formations and tensions in this relationship that make the study of globalization in a Russian context important for our understanding of the nature of the process. But applying globalization theories, which have mainly been formed on evidence from the West and the developing nations, to the case of post-Communist Russia, reveals major gaps.

MEDIA AND GLOBALIZATION: IMPERIALISM

Traditionally, media and communication scholars have emphasized the conflict between the global and the national, which is seen most clearly in the media imperialism (or cultural imperialism) debate. Its participants were pioneers, the first-generation globalization theorists in media and communication studies. They were the first to notice that media and communications played a significant role globally, but their main concern was the inequality in communication structures, rather than the individual experiences studied by later theorists. The processes of globalization and nationalism were seen as discrete, even antagonistic, toward each other, instead of being part of the same process.

The starting point for globalization and nationalism was that media and communications between nations (as the term "international" communication implies) were in an unequal relationship. Oliver Boyd-Barrett defined media imperialism as "the process whereby the ownership, structure, distribution or content of the media in any one country are singly or together subject to substantial external pressures from media interests of any other country or countries without proportionate reciprocation of influence by the country so affected" (1977, 117). He himself later noted the weaknesses of the media imperialism concept. Among them was the assumption that nation-states are the basic building blocks within the field of global media activities, and that there is a simple association between particular media and particular countries. Boyd-Barrett writes, "Because media systems are often complex hybrids of different agencies and actors, it is not advisable to make simple identification of whole corporations with particular national identities—this is precisely why we need to take account of the multidimensionality of media activity" (1998, 167–68). Media imperialism scholars tended to identify the ownership of media institutions and the content of their products with U.S. imperialism. Studies of the development of global media have indicated otherwise—the boundaries between ownership, structure, distribution, or content are so overlapped and blurry that it is often almost impossible to say what the country of origin of a particular media product is. This is precisely the point that Tomlinson makes about globalization—it is much less culturally directed than media imperialism theories imply (1991, 175).

The second point Boyd-Barrett raises is important, because it reminds us that even national media systems are not homogenous blocks consisting of perfectly balanced elements. There are different kinds of national media systems in which discrete parts have developed unevenly. Even in totalitarian media systems, such as that of the Soviet Union, some parts of the media and communication system were technologically advanced (television, for example), while others hardly existed (new communications technology).

The media imperialism model further assumes that it is in the interests of one country to reject or oppose media imperialism of another country in the name of national interest. Again, there is often no single national interest, but separate media enterprises, which compete against each other both nationally and globally. As John Sinclair et al. observe about global television, the imperialism thesis did not consider the strategic social and structural position of the individuals and interest groups who benefited from facilitating U.S. market entry or even from taking their own initiatives (1996, 9). Some individuals and interest groups have subsequently built up their own national and global media empires. In post-Communist Russia different media barons struggle over the control of the domestic television market by forming alliances with domestic and foreign partners.

Boyd-Barrett's fourth critique of the media imperialism argument was that it did not take into account the question of the audience, but concentrated solely on the production process. Experience of the media was beyond the scope of such research or was considered a homogenous phenomenon. Sinclair et al. note that the imperialism theory tended to identify the United States as the single center of a process of media-centric capitalist influence that flowed outward to the rest of the world in the form of television programs (1996, 179–80). It assumed that these programs had an inevitable and self-sufficient ideological effect upon their helpless audiences in the periphery. It presupposed that audiences did not really want to have U.S. or Western programs, but were somehow seduced into watching them. In the Soviet and post-Soviet context, media imperialism scholars must confront the unthinkable—Russian audiences actually wanted to have Western programs, to which they were denied access for decades.

The case of post-Communist Russia offers further conundrums to media imperialism theory. The Soviet Union was a formidable exporter of films and television and radio programs to certain other countries. Statistics for the 1970s and early 1980s show that the Soviet Union was the largest purveyor of broadcast information in the world. Its broadcasting schedule each week included 2,010 hours in eighty different languages, some of which, such as Quechua, are spoken by a very small minority of people (Ellis 1998, 210). The Soviet Union itself practiced a version of media or cultural imperialism—not through the ownership of its media, but through its political presence in other communist countries. Admittedly, this was a different form of imperialism, but it had an influence that is still felt, because what post-Communist Russia has inherited is the aftermath of its consequences, one of which is the deimperialization of the Soviet psyche (Wyman 1997, 172).

The tables have been turned, and the country faces the problems of other countries that are exposed to exogenous media and communications. At the same time, its response to new conditions is quite different to that of a developing nation, or of the Central and Eastern European nations. Compared to developing nations, post-Communist Russia already had a media and communications system in place, in which the old technologies (such as television or radio) are relatively well developed, although the new (latest communication technology) are behind the most advanced countries. Compared to other postcommunist countries, Russia is a former superpower, once an exporter of television programs that held considerable political and financial influence in other communist countries. Richard Collins directed attention to the role of English as the language of advantage—the first language of television films and serials—referring to the size and wealth of the market that makes English more advantageous compared to other languages (1990, 211). As he further observed, English is a potential language of production (which may or may not be realizable), rather than a necessary language. When Communism collapsed, the major political hindrance to the liberalization of the trade of television programs was abolished, and English rapidly replaced Russian as the language of advantage in televisions films and serials in Central and Eastern Europe.

One can also say that the Russian language once enjoyed a somewhat similar position to English as a language of advantage when the Soviet Union held superpower status and a dominant position in Eastern Europe. Its *position* as a major exporter of television programs was not based on successful trade, but on its political mission as the leading Communist country. Programs were not sold at a profitable price, but were practically given away for free. Simultaneously, the Iron Curtain successfully prevented the import of Western programs, and of the English language, for several decades. After the collapse of Communism, Russian became the language of disadvantage, and there was no demand for Russian programs in Central and Eastern Europe. The advantage it previously held had become unattainable in the new circumstances. The loss of that status, combined with the size of the country and its population, makes post-Communist Russia stand in a league of its own.

MEDIA AND GLOBALIZATION: MEDIATION

If the imperialism theories have mainly concentrated on the structures or contents of media, globalization theories have paid much attention to individual experience. Giddens observes that, although everybody lives a local life, phenomenal worlds for the most part are truly global (1991, 187). What this implies is that although the intersection between presence and absence takes place in a specific locality, there is nevertheless a difference between local and global experience. Obviously, we cannot physically be in two places at the same time, although improved transportation reduces time taken to travel between two places. Media, particularly television, however, allows us to experience being in two places at the same time—the location in which we watch a television program about a second, distant location. Ulrich Beck uses the concept of *place polygamy* to describe belonging to different worlds—a marriage to several places at once (2000, 73). However, for most Russians, place polygamy outside the Soviet Union became available only after the collapse of Communism, when traveling was permitted. Still, for most Russians, media are the main sources of having access to several places at once. As Tomlinson aptly concludes, "Organizations are the prime instance of the potential for the reintegration of time and space which is characteristic of modernity—once time and space are separated from the constraints of presence availability, their recombination in organizations (including nation-states) produces the dynamic mode of life we recognize as the modern world" (1994, 151). As Giddens puts it, "Modern organizations are able to connect the local and the global in ways which would have been unthinkable in more traditional societies, and in doing so, routinely affect the lives of millions of people" (1990, 20). Among these modern organizations are those of media and communications, often perceived as technologies, rather than as organizations, by scholars outside media studies.

A key concept in understanding the role of media and communications in globalization, according to Tomlinson's (1994, 155) interpretation of Giddens, is mediation. It is generally acknowledged that all of our experiences are mediated through language, but being here and there at the same time is mostly a mass-mediated experience, in contrast to everyday, shared experiences. Tomlinson distinguishes between mass-mediated and non-mass mediated experiences (1994, 157). The latter is very similar to Thompson's mediated quasi-interaction (1995, 84), or Harvey's mass-mediated social relationships (1993, 14). Mass-mediated experiences largely, if not solely, mediate media and communications. Their presence in contemporary, everyday life is probably the most distinctive feature compared to traditional societies. Media offer mass-mediated experience to people in the world who would otherwise only live their local lives.

Thompson and Tomlinson emphasize that mass-mediated and non-mass mediated experiences are not the same. They both note that mediated quasi-interaction or mass-mediated experiences are monological in character, in the sense that the flow of communication is predominantly one-way (Thompson 1995, 35–36), or lacks dialogue (Tomlinson 1994, 158, 168). Hence, although people live more globally through mass-mediated experience, their global and local experiences differ from each other. By its nature, media offer one-way experiences that are consumed in localities by audiences, not by members of the global community (Tomlinson 1994, 169). Tomlinson emphasizes that the consumption of a media program is a shared experience, but not in the same way as a communal experience, because it lacks the facility of talking back.

A great merit of this approach is that it pays attention to the role of individual experience. What is missing in this analysis, however, is a consideration of structures and contents. Although Giddens and Tomlinson both note the influence of institutions, they are not given sustained attention that risks portraying media solely as mediators or connectors, and neglects their structures. Whereas media imperialism occupies one extreme position (a homogenous media content forced upon all citizens in all locations), the scholars of the globalization of experience theory occupy the other extreme in their vision of media as links of experiences. The relationship between media organizations and the communications that produce the substance of experiences rarely gets attention.

MEDIA AND GLOBALIZATION: NATIO-GLOBALIZATION

Media imperialism theory paid attention to the homogeneity of programs available around the world. First-generation globalization theorists in media studies were much more interested in structures, while the second generation of theorists concentrated on audiences. Not surprisingly, heterogenization or hybridization concepts have replaced those of homogenization and other similar concepts in recent theoretical discussions. As Chris Barker notes, "discussion of diaspora identities and hybridization raise the issue of 'reverse flows', the impact of non-Western ideas and practices on the West" (1997, 203). His examples include the import of telenovelas from Latin America to other countries of the world, the global impact of reggae, hip-hop, and world music, the influence of Islam and other religions, and the commodification and sale of ethnic food and clothing within the West. Evidence of reverse flows contradicts imperialism assumptions that cultural products mainly flow from the United States to other countries, and suggests the interpenetration of the global into the local and the local into the global.

Robertson uses the term glocalization to describe the simultaneity and the interpenetration of what are conventionally called the global and the local (1995, 29–31). Media and communications have increased interconnectedness, or connectivity as Tomlinson calls it (1999, 175). What is missing here is a reconsideration of the recombination of the global and the national. It is not only the global and the local that cross over, but the national and the global as well. In contrast to imperialism theories, the result is not necessarily homogenization. According to Robertson, we should be careful not to equate the communicative and interactional connecting of such cultures—including very asymmetrical forms of such communications and interaction, as well as "third" cultures of mediation—with the notion of homogenization of all cultures. He emphasizes that what is needed is an understanding of the two seemingly opposing trends: homogenization and heterogenization, both of which are present in globalization (1995, 31, 40).

What also follows from the intersection of the global, the national, and the local is the plurality of reactions to globalization. This notion is crucial for the purpose of this book. Featherstone distinguishes absorption/assimilation/resistance strategies in relationship to globalization. He writes:

> In the first place it is apparent that once we investigate actual cases the situation is exceedingly complex. It is not just a question of the everyday practical culture of local inhabitants giving way to globally marketed products. Such market culture/local culture interactions are mediated by the nation state, which in the process of creating a national identity will educate and employ its own range of cultural specialists and intermediaries. . . . Hence, depending on the priority it

gives to the nation-forming processes, it can reinvent memories, traditions and practices with which to resist, channel or control market penetration. (1995, 116)

Featherstone's observation again brings national media systems into the picture as intermediaries between globalization and people's experiences. Instead of concentrating only on the audience, we can also study media institutions and their adjustment to the processes of globalization. In the same way, as strategies of absorption/assimilation/resistance vary among people, they also vary among media institutions. In addition to these reactions, there could be acceptance, indifference, or hostility. This is what the media imperialism debate neglected. In post-Communist Russia all these strategies are available, but how they are actually used, not only by Russian audiences but also by media and communications as national institutions in the era of globalization, is the topic of this book.

Not only did people's experiences change slowly in Russia, but the nature of institutions changed as well. The collapse of Communism is sometimes perceived as a total breakdown of the old system. In reality, the transition has been an interplay of the old and the new, where new structures emerge but many of the old structures still remain. The present Russian media and communications system follows the same pattern—there is something old (such as parts of news agencies and television), something new (such as parts of new communications technology), something borrowed (such as imported Western advertising) and something blue (such as the unexpected formations between the old and the new). The old and the new do not necessarily follow the boundaries of different media sectors, but often take place inside them (for example, within state-owned and commercial television channels), and form alliances with other sectors (for example, video with new communications technology). Sometimes the changes go hand in hand with each other, but sometimes they conflict with each other. The interplay between the national and the global takes place in the structures and contents that are partly inherited from the past, partly imported from abroad. The evolving new national media, as well as people's experience, reflect this in-between status. Changes in experience and structures do not necessarily take place simultaneously and do not move in the same direction.

This book investigates the development of post-Soviet media and communications in a newly globalized environment following radical social change. Through the examination of four different case studies, this book analyzes the junctures of the global and the national, the new and the old, media and communications, and production and consumption. These case studies have been deliberately chosen—they represent the old, and the new, media and communications. The old are news agencies, television, and old communications technology, such as the telephone. News agencies were founded in Imperial Russia. Television was developed and reached maturity in the Soviet period. The new media are advertising and new communications technology, such as the Internet. Advertising and new media and communications were born after the collapse of Communism, and thus have no history in the Communist era.

To preface this investigation, the next chapter describes the development of the Russian media system and how it has changed since the collapse of Communism.

2

Media and Communications Systems in Russia

Globalization does not take place in a vacuum but interacts with national media systems. It is misleading to think that globalization "spills like soup," because the different forms and stages of globalization are very much dependent on the forms and stages of development of national media systems. In post-Communist Russia, the media and communications system is changing radically, with the process of globalization acting unevenly and incompletely. Media systems engage with other systems in the cultural landscape. Appadurai identifies five dimensions of global cultural flow consisting of (a) ethnoscapes; (b) mediascapes; (c) technoscapes; (d) financescapes; and (e) ideoscapes. For him, current global culture flows in and through the growing disjunctures between the five different scapes (1990, 6–7, 11). In post-Communist Russia, all these scapes are simultaneously on the move, as discussed in chapter 1. There are junctures and disjunctures not only among the different scapes, but also within the different parts of the Russian mediascape.

Globalization takes a different form on each scape or part of the scape. If the system (or parts of it) is relatively developed, as in Western Europe or in the United States, the effects of globalization are quite different to those of post-Soviet Russia. Some media systems have been exposed to globalization for longer periods of time, while postcommunist countries entered the age of globalization late and suddenly (although there were some communist countries such as Estonia and Hungary that had already been exposed to globaliza-

19

tion). The very quality of discontinuity characterizes the process of globalization in Russia.

Before exploring the Russian mediascape, the components of a national media system must be identified. Traditionally, a media system is defined through different media industries. For example, Kaarle Nordenstreng and Osmo A. Wiio describe a media system as a collection of subsystems consisting of institutions of production and delivery (1994). The authors include newspapers, magazines, news transmission, radio, television, cable and satellite television, literature, public libraries, film and video, recording, advertising, telecommunications, and even media economics and legislation as components of the system (Nordenstreng and Wiio 1986; 1994). Media systems, as defined thus, can also include communications technology, since the transmission of messages takes place with the help of technology, and the audience. Without doubt, this definition implies an existence of a mass audience.

This book, however, adopts a slightly different approach. Although the division between the media (traditionally referring to technology, ownership, content, and audience) and communications (traditionally referring mainly to technology) has become more and more blurred because of convergence, it is important to make a distinction between media and communications. On the one hand, in Russia, there is a national mass media system in which the ownership, contents, and audience remain partly national. On the other hand, there is a national communications system where ownership, contents, and audience are becoming more and more global, and which consists of not just mass communication, but of interpersonal communication (such as the telephone or e-mail) as well. In the Soviet Union, government and the Communist Party controlled the national mass media and communications systems. In contrast to mass media, however, interpersonal communications could not be entirely controlled. When Appadurai talks about junctures and disjunctures between the scapes, we can also talk about junctures and disjunctures between media and communications. Globalization does not enter media and communications simultaneously, and media and communications in turn respond to globalization in distinct ways.

Historically, national mass media systems in general began with the development of a national press, and as Anderson notes, the press played a significant role in promoting nationalism (1983). Other components to national media systems—broadcasting, for example—were added as communications technology developed. Unlike the printed media, broadcasting developed early in Soviet Russia; it was evolved under strict state and party guidance. In the early 1920s, Soviet broadcasting served the ideological needs of the newly established nation, and, until Communism collapsed, the state-owned and party-controlled media were virtually insulated against the effects of globalization.

It is also important to note that a Russian media and communications system has a history that goes back to Imperial Russia. As Elena Vartanova (2000) has pointed out, present-day Russian media structures, along with the media-power paradigm, integrated traditions of the pre-revolutionary Russian press when they were transformed during the fall of Communism. In Imperial Russia, the most distinctive feature of the printed medium was its extraordinary lateness. The first regular periodical was established in 1727, long after those of developed European countries of the time. The tradition of "official" periodicals, referring to journals or newspapers that were either owned, controlled, or financed by the government, was the longest-standing tradition in Russian journalism. Although, in the 1860s, Russian newspapers entered a new phase of mass-produced commercialization, the country still lacked a legal "party press" (or organs of political parties), which did not make its appearance until 1905, still under Tsarist censorship. The existence of numerous censorship statutes (1804, 1826, 1828, 1848, 1865, 1879, 1882), before preliminary censorship was abolished after the "bourgeois" revolution in 1917, shows that the commercial press was censored throughout its existence (Vartanova 2000). News agencies—the first electronic medium of the nineteenth century—soon also became controlled and then owned by the state (Rantanen 1990, 59–70). When Yassen Zassoursky (2000) identifies statism and commercialization as the major characteristics of Russian media and communications in the beginning of the twenty-first century, Vartanova (2000) refers to the long-standing tradition that already started in Imperial Russia.

The Soviet media system was one of the most nationalist, because both the ownership and content were almost entirely domestic. This had not always been the case, however. The daily press in early-twentieth-century Imperial Russia bears similarity (with the exception of

censorship) to its counterparts—universal press in other countries—
and the first Russian news agency was established at the same time
as other national agencies (Rantanen 1990). The 1917 October Revolution interrupted this development. When the Bolsheviks seized all
strategic points in St. Petersburg, including railway stations, bridges,
the telephone company, and the national bank, they also captured
the telegraph agency. Two days later the Military Revolutionary
Committee issued a decree that forbade the publication of "bourgeois and counter-revolutionary newspapers." Further, it confiscated
the agency's paper supply, machinery, and buildings (Rantanen
1994, 8). This was the beginning of the closed national media system
that exemplified the Soviet period.

Closed national media systems in communist countries were isolated from exchanges with the noncommunist West. Because the state
and the party owned the media, it was possible to control the media
fully. Thus, the media operated as filters against dangerous Western
influence on citizens. The task of the Soviet media system was to promote three things: communism, nationalism, and proletarian internationalism. Although communism was, in theory, ideologically
opposed to nationalism, in practice a kind of nationalism was promoted as a part of it—the Soviet Union was superior to capitalist
countries and took the leadership among communist countries. The
global element present in the Soviet Union at this time was internationalism, but it was restricted to the exchange with other communist
countries and "progressive forces" in the West.

The Soviet media system had a special position compared to other
communist countries. Because the nation was a union consisting of
fifteen republics, was the leading communist country, and the second
strongest superpower in the world, its media had specific functions.
First, the media were to promote the Soviet way of life and defend
the structure of the Soviet Union. Second, they were to spread Soviet
supremacy among other communist countries. Third, the media
were to promote international proletarianism. Some of its media
were international, for example, TASS (Telegraph Agency of the
Soviet Union), which was the fifth largest news agency in the world.
Soviet radio was also international, in that it broadcast around the
world. Both had an important countertask as bulwarks against Western propaganda that threatened the existence of the Communist
system.

To be able to fulfill its tasks, the media system had to be controlled, centralized, and vertical. Control was exercised through party control, official state censorship, hierarchical appointments, and self-censorship (Paasilinna 1995, 98). Centralization operated through concentration of the media in Moscow, from where messages were transmitted to other parts of the country. Every republic had its own media organizations that were structured in the same way as the headquarters in Moscow. Thus, the government news agency TASS had its headquarters in Moscow, but every republic had its own TASS office located in its capital. The leading communist newspaper, *Pravda,* was at the top of the vertical hierarchy, followed by other national, regional, and local newspapers, in order of importance. This strictly organized system was governed from a single center— the Central Committee of the Communist Party (Y. Zassoursky 1998, 15). Broadcasting followed the same principles: there were two Moscow-based channels to broadcast programs in Russian to the fifteen Soviet republics (Mickiewicz 1997, 24).

Ellen Mickiewitcz adds another important characteristic of the Soviet media system—saturation (1997, 25, 27). She uses the term in two senses—first, the political leadership sought total penetration of the potential audience; second, the approved message pattern and content were to thoroughly infuse the output of the media, purveying a single party line and eliminating the possibility of countermessages. The elimination of countermessages, mainly from abroad, became one of the key functions of the Soviet media system. This is the main reason why globalization started much later in Russia than in other countries. The measures for eliminating countermessages included the jamming of foreign broadcasts, having different FM radio frequency bands from the West, selecting a different television transmission standard from that of the closest European neighboring countries, and preventing the import of typing machines, cassettes, et cetera (Paasilinna 1995, 129).

As a result, the Soviet mass media system could not meet the expectations of large parts of its audience. Alternative communications, such as *samizdat* (underground literature) or illegally copied cassettes, mushroomed in the shadow of the big media system. Foreign radio stations such as Voice of America and *Deutsche Welle* were available to Russians, although their use was restricted by radio wave jamming and penalization. Alternative communications provided the global elements in Soviet society. And, in the later years of the Communist period, there was an increasing demand for these global elements, which came predominantly from the West.

THE TRANSFORMATION OF
THE OLD MEDIA SYSTEM

When a societal system collapses, what happens to its media system? According to Colin Sparks, in Central and Eastern Europe the changes in broadcasting begun by the collapse of the old system were followed by the introduction of new broadcasting laws (1995, 12–13). The situation in post-Communist Russia was not so simple. In post-Communist Russia, media laws are still incomplete. The Soviet media system did not collapse overnight, but it underwent, and is still undergoing, a long process in which different parts of the old system changed, and continue to change, at different paces. There were also aspects of the Soviet media system that were relatively well developed, such as television or radio, while others were less developed, such as the telephone. Moreover, new types of media and communications were being born. In the old Soviet Union, advertising and new media did not exist. Ivan Zassoursky (2000) divides the development of the Soviet/post-Communist Russian media system into five different periods, consisting of (1) Soviet (1920–1985); (2) glasnost-oriented propaganda machine (1986–1990); (3) fourth power, independent media (1991–1995); (4) economic-political (1996–2000); and (5) "Great Russia" (2000–). In each period, Zassoursky looks at, among other things, structures, ideology, change, means of control, and opposition. I find his divisions useful, but I would also suggest minor changes. I. Zassoursky (2000) suggests that globalization takes place only in the fourth period—spectacle society—but I would argue that it started earlier.

Glasnost-Oriented Propaganda, 1986–1990

The first wave of transformation began in 1985–1986 with the start of *perestroika*, when the contents of the media started to change. Initially, the main issues in the press were criticism of Stalinism, the administrative and bureaucratic state system, and support for new political and economic movements. Several old newspapers such as

Table 2.1 Media Systems in the Soviet Union and Russia, 1920–2000

System	Soviet	Glasnost-oriented Propaganda Machine	Independent Media	Spectacle Society	"Great Russia"
Historical period	1920–1985	1986–1990	1991–1995	1996–2000	2000–
Importance of mediums	1. Newspaper 2. Radio 3. TV	1. Newspaper 2. TV 3. Radio	1. TV 2. Newspaper 3. Radio	1. TV 2. Radio 3. Newspaper	1. TV 2. Radio 3. Newspaper
Bias	Ideological, strong persuasion, and manipulation	Ideological, soft persuasion	Strong persuasion	Strong manipulation	Strong persuasion and manipulation
Change	New media system introduced by coercion and as a part of the new social project.	Unprecedented increase in printed media circulation, first live broadcasts of political events and news shown on TV. First advertisements.	New media law guarantees freedom of expression, media become independent. Printed media start losing their circulation due to high prices of paper and delivery. Advertising increases rapidly. Film industry in serious decline.	Chain ownership. Sophisticated manipulative techniques are introduced. Media become commercialized. Satellite and Internet are introduced. Economic crisis decreases advertising.	State becomes the dominating power center. Commercial media and Internet boom. Internet offers a promise of counter-culture.
Means of Control	Party and state	Party and state plus alliance	Capital plus alliance	Politicized capital	State and politicized capital
Opposition	Oral communication. Samizdat and foreign media (radio and printed media).	Radical, samizdat, conservative Communist, and foreign media. Video.	Communist and nationalist newspapers.	Communist, nationalist, and alternative newspapers.	NTV and other Gusinky media, alternative media, Internet, and foreign media.

Source: I. Zassoursky 2000 (modified).

Moscow News, an official paper aimed at foreigners, and *Argumenty i Fakty*, a former Communist Party propaganda paper, changed their editorial policy and became strong supporters of *perestroika*. This period also witnessed the appearance of small, periodic, and informal newspapers whose number grew quickly. They did not last very long, but were very popular at the time. Along with newspapers that had already undergone reforms, these informal publications comprised the alternative independent press (Vartanova 1991, 7).

Individual projects in electronic media expanded the range of political topics and programs, thereby posing a direct challenge to dominant journalistic practices. Critical journalism—such as attacks on Stalinism and bureaucratic abuses—together with support for new political and economic movements, made their way into radio and television programs. The political range of old programs broadened and new political programs appeared. For example, *Vzgliad* (Viewpoint), a late-night weekend show, contained rock and pop music and light cultural issues, but focused mainly on political discussions with former dissidents, army generals, young radicals, and anti-Communists—all of whom had not been previously allowed on television (Vartanova 1991, 11). In 1987, Soviet television showed a live ABC broadcast of the satellite *Space Bridge*, entitled "Capital to Capital," which transmitted discussions between Soviet and American citizens. These discussions were found to be of great significance and contributed to positive attitudes toward U.S. citizens among Soviet citizens (Paasilinna 1995, 135). The live transmissions from the First Congress of People's Deputies in 1989 became a symbol of glasnost in programming policy. Viewers followed the session in a state of "open-mouthed excitement." Production fell by 20 percent in work places during the telecasts (Paasilinna 1995, 146).

It was not only domestically produced programs that were changing, however. The official attitude toward foreign programming became more relaxed. Unofficially, ordinary people had access to Western films and music through video- and audiocassettes. The trade in cassettes became open and public. Listening to previously banned Western radio stations became tolerated, and the Soviet Union stopped jamming Western radio broadcasts after the Reykjavik summit meeting of 1987 (Paasilinna 1995, 135).

The first wave of globalization coincided with the arrival of commercialization, itself a response to the economic problems of *Gostel-*

eradio, the state-owned broadcasting company. The commercial response resulted in the birth of a new medium—advertising. Previously, television was financed by the state but, with financial cuts and increased demands for the modernization of transmitting equipment, the broadcasting company turned to advertising. Soviet viewers saw their first American television advertisements in 1987 during the live ABC broadcast of the *Space Bridge*. Following the television program *Vzgliad* in 1987, many television programs began placing a commercial between various program segments. The Soviet Channel One ran its first advertisements in 1988 (Mickiewicz 1997, 232). On New Year's Eve, 1989, advertising interrupted a film on Soviet television for the first time (Kolesnik 1991, 51).

Advertising, however, grew slowly. In 1988, Soviet television received 2.5 billion rubles from the state budget, and made only 22 million rubles by itself (Androunas 1993, 118). Initially, advertising met an enthusiastic reception. The trademark of the Italian corporation *Olivetti* appeared on the face of the clock that counted the last minutes and seconds before the major national evening news program of that time (*Vremia*), without any criticism. Elena Androunas calls this the *Olivettization* of *Vremia* (Androunas 1993, 119, 122).

Advertising was not the only imported cultural product. The German magazine *Burda*, which began to be translated into Russian in 1987, immediately achieved a huge success among Russian women (Iampol'skaia and Serkova 1998, 118). *Burda* gave Russian women access to Western fashion by publishing not only photographs of clothes, but also instructions on how to make them, thus filling a demand that had been ignored by the old Soviet media.

The first private news agencies—Postfactum (established in 1987) and Interfax (established in 1989)—started to operate in this period. Both agencies started to use small communications technology methods as an alternative to the big and expensive technology controlled by the state. They used messengers, faxes, and e-mail, and soon gained a reputation, especially among foreigners, as alternative agencies (especially Interfax) delivering news that was not available from TASS, the official agency.

Fourth Power, Independent Media, 1991–1995

The Law on the Press and Other Media, which guaranteed the freedom of the press and prohibited censorship, came into force in 1990 and lasted until the beginning of 1992, when it was replaced by the Statute on Mass Media (Y. Zassoursky 1998, 82; Richter 2000). The Law on Press and Other Media established the inadmissibility of censorship, and included the basic provisions for the freedom of information: for seeking, obtaining, producing, and disseminating information. It also allowed private broadcasting and prohibited the ownership (founding) of mass media by foreign citizens—but not by foreign companies (Richter 2000). As Andrei Richter remarks, the media law in Russia has been a revolution that has laid the foundation for the present Russian democracy.

What is known as the first stage of privatization started after the adoption of the Media Law. It was marked by the establishment of national daily newspapers, including *Nezavisimiaia gazeta* (Independent Newspaper), *Megapolis Express* (Metropolitan Express) and *Kommersant* (Businessman), as well as television channels and radio stations, all independent of political parties or movements. This increased commercialization of the media was closely connected with the economic reforms and privatization that took place in the country generally. If politics had been the main issue in the mass media during the earlier phase of *perestroika*, the economy now emerged as a central focus of concern.

Although a few small private media companies had already begun to operate before 1990, such as the first small cable television organizations, and the private NIKA-TV in 1989 (Ganley 1996, 76; Paasilinna 1995, 157), this second period saw a more widespread establishment of new television companies. The reorganization of Russian central television began in 1990, when the state-owned Russian television station RTR (Russian Television and Radio) was founded. RTR started broadcasting in April 1991, and started to show its programs on the Second Channel. In November 1994 President Yeltsin signed a decree "privatizing" the Ostankino Broadcasting Company, with the government owning 51 percent of the shares. The new entity, called Russian Public Television (ORT), took control and was responsible for programs on the First Channel from January 1, 1995 ("Yeltsin Approves Ostankino Privatization" 1994). The first non-governmental television company, the commercial Telekanal 2x2, was founded in 1990. Its entertainment-oriented programming was directed at the Moscow area and became quite popular—its establishment was followed by about thirty similar companies (Paasilinna 1995, 141). As Mickiewitcz writes, "All over Russia—in locales, in apartment buildings, in pockets of homes linked by cable—small television stations began popping up" (1997, 221). Although the first private television channel appeared as early as 1990, the first private national channel, NTV (Independent Television), began its operations in 1993, and became the Fourth Channel.

Unlike other postcommunist countries, such as the German Democratic Republic (GDR) or Hungary, where foreign companies took over the printed media market, Russian media remained mainly in domestic ownership. Russia is one of the few countries in Eastern Europe where foreign investment has not played a key role in the growth of media. One exception was in the press, where 51 percent of *Pravda* was bought by a Greek publisher (Androunas 1993, 67). A remarkable new phenomenon was that of global magazines published in the Russian language. In 1992, a Dutch company, Independent Media, was founded to publish and distribute magazines and newspapers such as the *Moscow Times*. In 1994, Independent Media and Hearst Magazines International started to publish Russian-language editions of magazines such as *Cosmopolitan* and *Good Housekeeping*. Later, Independent Media published *Marie Claire* in Russian, in partnership with the Marie Claire Group, and a Russian *Playboy* with Playboy Enterprises (Mironenko and Mironenko 1998, 114–15). There was very little foreign ownership of Russian electronic media; the few exceptions were the French partial ownership of the radio stations Nostalgie and Europe Plus, and the American partial ownership of Radio Maximum (Androunas 1993, 121). The first independent broadcast television station, TV-6, began as a joint venture with the Turner Broadcasting System in 1993, but in 1994 Turner and TV-6 dissolved their partnership (Mickiewicz 1997, 222).

In contrast, electronic media contents became increasingly global. The new cable channels were filled with pirated videos, movies, animated cartoons, and local advertising without their own programming (Androunas 1993, 111). The major globalization of television programs took place on the former state-owned national terrestrial channels. When the state television started to show the Mexican soap opera *The Rich Also Cry* in 1992, to fill the vacuum between the sessions of the Congresses of the People's Deputies, it consistently headed the Top Ten Programs. It was estimated that 70 percent of the population tuned in regularly. As the *Moscow Times* reported: "When the film started, the streets became desolate, crowds gathered in stores selling TV sets, tractors stopped in the fields and guns fell silent on the Azerbaijani-Armenian front" (Baldwin 1995, 285–86). The program had to be shown twice a day in order to avoid a precipitous drop in labor productivity (Borenstein 1999, 55). Market research showed that some 43 percent of Moscow's population watched every episode of *The Rich Also Cry*. Across the territory of the former Soviet Union, viewers were estimated at some one hundred million (Ellis 1998, 220). In 1994, the most popular soap opera was again Latin American, this time *Just Maria* (Borenstein 1999, 55).

It was during this period that the printed press started to decline. Within the Russian system, there has been an important shift from print to electronic media. In the Soviet period, the joint circulation of the central newspapers amounted to one hundred million copies daily, but in 1991–1992, the circulation of the most popular dailies reached only twenty to twenty-four million copies. All print circulations started to drop consistently. According to Y. Zassoursky, the decline evoked serious concerns about the future of the press, especially daily newspapers (1998, 16–21). The drift from print to electronic media is a crucial feature not only of the national media system itself, but also of the national media system's globalization.

Spectacle Society, 1996–2000

The disappearance of party control not only opened the door to privatization, but also to commercial concentration. As Vartanova notes, Russia has its own media moguls who own chains of media (1997, 19). In some cases, banks have become media owners. For example, the MOST group controls the Russian national television channel NTV, the radio station *Ekho Moskvy*, and the news magazine *Itogy*. In other cases, it is the government or Moscow City that has achieved control over various media. For example, Moscow City controls the television channel TV Centre, and various newspapers and journals. In comparison to their Western counterparts, Russian media moguls' activities are mainly limited by national boundaries. What are also particularly true in Russia are the media barons' close connections with ruling politicians and their involvement in politics. I. Zassoursky calls this phenomenon "politicized capital," when the new Russian business elite rushed to invest in media, taking over traditional independent publications and entertainment television (2000). According to I. Zassoursky, the political parties (except Communists) are weak without mass membership or grassroot support, and have become election brands. As a result, the role of the parties was determined by media holdings. As Sparks observes, the alignment of different sections of the capital with various political forces can be understood as an effort by the political element to gain access to sources of funding, and by the economic element to secure a position of advantage in the competitive struggle (2000a, 42). The declining revenues from advertising markets have further enforced this development. In this situation, where the media are more and more dependent on advertising, any decline in revenues forces the media to look for other alternatives. During elections, media become more and more dependent on the political advertising market. Consequently, as I. Zassoursky and Vartanova (2000) note, political advertising is the only truly reliable source of media that remains.

Politicized capital, together with increasing dependence on political advertising, can be seen especially in television. Although the 1996 presidential election is often considered the turning point, Mickiewitcz (1999, 135) points out that since the referendum election of 1993, television has played a critical role in affecting turnout and

Table 2.2   Soviet/Russian Newspapers, 1940–1998

Years	Titles	Issues	Daily circulation (thousands)	Total circulation (thousands)	Average daily circulation of an individual newspaper (thousands)
1940	5,730	604,268	25,156	5,094,619	4.4
1960	4,474	585,561	45,629	11,053,327	10.2
1980	4,413	502,822	119,574	29,245,100	27.1
1990	4,808	523,886	165,546	37,848,556	34.4
1998	5,436	395,764	112,483	7,505,715	20.7

Source: Vartanova 2000.

influencing voters' party preferences. In the campaign that preceded the referendum of April 25, 1993, on presidential/parliamentary standoff, television became for the first time mass medium Number One (Mickiewitcz 1999, 135). Also, there was a clear preponderance of the pro-presidential position on news and public affairs programs on the state-run television channels. Television revolutionized electoral campaigning by introducing political advertising imported from the United States. Yeltsin's campaign manager invited a U.S. advertising agency to design his campaign, and other candidates followed (Mickiewitcz 1999, 137–41). Mickiewitcz calls this the "Americanization" of the electoral campaigns in post-Communist Russia (1999, 189).

By 1995, both newspapers and television companies derived 30 to 50 percent of their budgets from advertising (Mickiewitcz 1997, 232). In 1998, Russia's television advertising market was worth at least two billion dollars (Dziadul 1998, 73). Gradually, advertising started provoking public controversy. As Mickiewitcz (1997, 234) puts it: "How could the emerging Russian national identity be detected in the plethora of foreign-made television shows?"(1997, 73). As early as in the spring of 1994, the deputy chief of Channel One remarked, "it is annoying that Russian television is beginning to speak primarily in English" (Mickiewitcz 1997, 235).

With the rapid increase of both national and local television channels (in 1998 there were 800 local companies), television has become the dominant medium. This development has several implications. One of them is that the television audience has also become more fragmented. At the same time, programming length has rapidly increased. When the political obstacles that prevented the import of foreign programs disappeared, television became the major medium of globalization. As Karol Jakubowicz observes, when national or local politics become a matter of serious disagreement, imported television programs become a convenient way to fulfill programming time (1997, 4). Imported programs have increased the amount of entertainment, not only on television, but with other media—including the press—as well.

In this period, new communications technologies (NCT) appeared in Russia, though they developed slowly compared to other countries. Russia was ranked 35th on the list of access to NCT per inhabitant in 1998. The number of online digital media, PCs, and mobile phones were very low, even compared to other postcommunist countries. Of the four million Russian computers, only 15 to 20 percent were installed in homes. If the media in the Communist period was concentrated in Moscow, so were the new media of this period. Moscow dominated many sectors of the market because 80 percent of financial resources are concentrated there (Y. Zassoursky and Vartanova 1999, 326).

"Great Russia," 2000–

In the 1996 presidential election, television channels, despite their forms of ownership, had agreed to support Boris Yeltsin. According to Mickiewicz, it was said that television partisanship in the 1996 election was not so much about the larger issue of the return of dictatorship, or even of the protection of free speech, but about private advantage (1999, 170). She writes:

> In Russia, television electoral politics, with its emphasis on personalization drawing from both Soviet traditions and Western imports, played to a nation uncertain of its future and lacking the secondary associations that can act as brakes or firewalls. Though it is only one factor in this complex model, television, the most powerful medium and desired political asset, could well have retarded the development of the very political parties that render the electoral system effective. (1999, 189)

Mickiewicz's observation comes very close to I. Zassoursky's concept of politicized capital. However, if in the previous period, it looked like the media barons were the most powerful, the most recent period witnesses an increasing influence of the state and of

Table 2.3   Access to New Communication Technology in Russia

	Access at Home		Access at Work	
Communications Device	*Percentage*	*per thousand*	*Percentage*	*per thousand*
Fax modem	0.7	267	1.8	686
Local network	0.3	120	2.8	80
E-mail	0.6	215	1.7	671
Internet	0.7	270	1.7	669

Source: Y. Zassoursky and Vartanova 1999, 323.

those who control it. This development is the most visible in electoral campaigns. In 1999–2000, a few attempts by some channels were made to support other candidates, but at the end they all supported President Putin, at that time Yeltsin's nominated successor. Despite Putin's refusal to campaign in televised debates with other candidates, he nevertheless was the subject of intensive coverage on every channel; indeed, all major channels gave most of their airtime to Putin (Raskine 2000). Y. Zassoursky characterizes the present period by the growing influence of the state on the media and their increasing commercialization (2000). According to him, these etatist tendencies are reflected in the creation of the Ministry of Press, Television, and Communication, which consolidates the state structures and regulate media and communications. The Ministry is authorized to license broadcasting frequencies and to monitor the performance of printed media. It has also started legal proceedings toward two national television companies, and has issued reprimands to two newspapers. The Ministry has also tried to introduce control over the content of the Internet, but Putin has not supported these proposals. The growing state influence is also seen in the coverage of the Chechen war. Y. Zassoursky writes:

> Etatist approaches to media are counterproductive. They erode the very essence of the freedom of the press. They turn media into the tools of the government. They substitute responsibility by accountability to government officials from whom society seems to mean the state; to government officials who tend to disregard human rights of individuals, including the right that the government and the state are accountable to individual citizens. Finally, etatist approaches discredit the very notion of the responsible and free press. It creates barriers to the free flow of information, to the openness of society. (2000)

Both I. Zassoursky (2000) and Y. Zassoursky (2000) see nationalism as an increasing factor in present-day Russian society. I. Zassoursky writes about the celebration of nationalism combined with all the inherent ideology of global media culture, or mainstream media. Y. Zassoursky notes that democracy and the freedom of the press are increasingly replaced with such clichés as "law and order," "state," and "national interests."

The status of television has risen not only in relation to newspapers, but also in relation to national radio. There are numerous new radio stations, but fewer and fewer national ones. National radio stations are losing their popularity and are gradually being replaced by new local stations that mainly broadcast music. The popularity of foreign radio broadcasts is also increasing. Russian audiences once again are turning to the BBC or Radio Liberty to receive information they cannot get from Russian radio broadcasts or newspapers (Y. Zassoursky 1998, 24, 28). However, national television reaches 98 percent of the population; it is the only medium that directly reaches virtually the entire population. Y. Zassoursky notes that, in the Russian Federation, many towns do not receive Moscow daily newspapers that in the Soviet period were more popular in distant provinces than the local papers (1998, 24). Now, the tables have been turned, and it is television that has become much more important in localities.

As Y. Zassoursky and Vartanova note, one of the most characteristic features of current Russian television is the lack of programming resources (1999, 321). Although national television produces many programs, including film and music, it cannot meet the demands of an increasing airtime. As a result, many Russian broadcasting companies are buying foreign programs. The import of foreign programs is an important aspect of globalization that has fundamentally changed the national character of the Russian media system.

Y. Zassoursky remarks that the structural changes in Russian mass media have led to the end of the vertical organization characteristic of the Soviet system (1998, 15). The vertical organization was, of course, closely connected with the Communist Party and state control. Although there are areas where it has disappeared, such as the demise of *Pravda,* vertical organization remains a characteristic of the media system. State broadcasting, for example, has seen the birth of new national companies and thousands of local stations, but it still controls television channels. The All-Russian State-Run Television and Broadcasting Company (VGTRK), founded in 1990, employs some one hundred thousand staff. It runs two television channels (Russian Television and Radio, or RTR, and the Culture Channel), nationwide broadcasting facilities, Russia's two largest radio stations (Radio Rossii and Radio Mayak) and two news agencies (Information Telegraph Agency of Russia-TASS, or ITAR-TASS, and the Russian Information Agency, or RIA), as well as ninety regional television companies.

Although the Internet has grown relatively slowly in Russia compared to many countries, it shows recent exploding growth (Loukina 2000). The Internet is still available to not more than 2 percent of the Russian population, but the number of users has doubled since 1996, when the number was 2.5 million. Loukina also remarks that current statistics show the restructuring of geographical distribution of Internet users (2000). Earlier, the main areas were concentrated in central Russia, but they have since moved to Siberia, the Far East, and the Volga region.

THE RUSSIAN MEDIA AND COMMUNICATIONS SYSTEM

An overall analysis of the present Russian media system reveals that it consists of several parts that originate from different periods. The oldest are, of course, printed media, which have now lost ground to electronic media. This is one of the most fundamental changes that does not necessarily have much to do with the collapse of Communism, but is instead a global phenomenon, already familiar from other countries, and probably, as such, a consequence of globalization. The postcommunist circumstances made this change probably more dramatic than elsewhere, but ultimately the change would have taken place in the Soviet Union if it had continued to exist.

Although the features of the old system—centralization, party control, verticalization, and saturation—have encountered significant disruption, they have not disappeared altogether. The disappearance of party control had significant consequences for other features,

Table 2.4   Internet Users in Russia, 1996–1999

Year	Thousands of people
1996	406
1997	747
1998	1171
1999	2500

Source: Loukina 2000.

mainly for saturation. There is no longer a single communist ideological message that the media can deliver. Set against a global context that values media freedom and independence, the change to the Russian media system is fundamental, but not total. For example, after the 1917 Revolution, some elements, such as state-owned news agencies, remained in place. The two state-owned news agencies, ITAR-TASS and RIA, have maintained their old status, although there are several private agencies competing with them, the most important of which is the private Interfax. We can see the same phenomenon in Russian television, in which there is still considerable state ownership. Hence, it is fair to say that the present media system still carries traits of the old system. Those parts that were born after the collapse, such as new media or advertising, were less prone to the overall influence of the old system.

Electronic media also consist of both old and new elements. The oldest electronic media are news agencies that originate from the nineteenth century. They are followed by broadcasting and television from the Soviet propaganda machine period. They have all gone through significant changes in their ownership, market structure, and content. Only the most recent communication technology (such as the Internet or mobile phones) does not have a past in societies that preceded the Russian Federation. Advertising is another example of the new that did not exist in the Soviet Union, although it did not exist in the press in Imperial Russia. Still, its present form in electronic communication is entirely new.

We can also look at the Russian media and communications system in its entirety and see elements that are common to each of its different parts. One element is legislation, and in some cases the lack of it. As Andrei Richter has noted, since the adoption of the Media Statute by the Supreme Soviet of the Russian Federation in 1991, more than thirty statutes and dozens of decrees were put into force in Russia, thus affecting mass media. At the same time, the Russian legislative framework for the media still lacks important features, such as a statute on television and radio broadcasting (Richter 2000). Thus, media and communications legislation remains incomplete, and is usually behind actual changes. Whether this is good or bad for the development of the system is not always clear. What is most important for democracy and individual citizens is the Constitution of the Russian Federation, which guarantees every person freedom of thought and speech, guarantees freedom of mass information, and prohibits censorship (Article 29). This is historically entirely new, and its importance cannot be underestimated. For the first time, Russian citizens may experience these freedoms.

The privatization of certain parts of the Russian media system does not mean that there has been a complete change from state to private ownership. In Russia, we see both, often walking hand in hand. The two tendencies, the growing influence of the state and commercialization, which are traditionally considered to be opposite to each other, are both very much present in the Russian media and communications system. Their coexistence, although sometimes contradictory, as we shall later see, is one of the consequences of globalization.

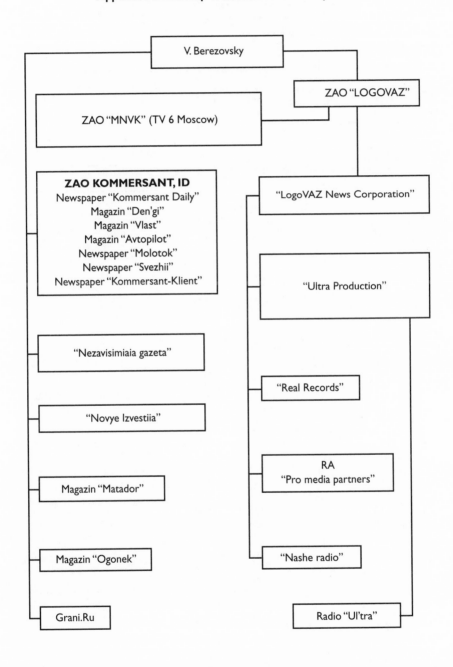

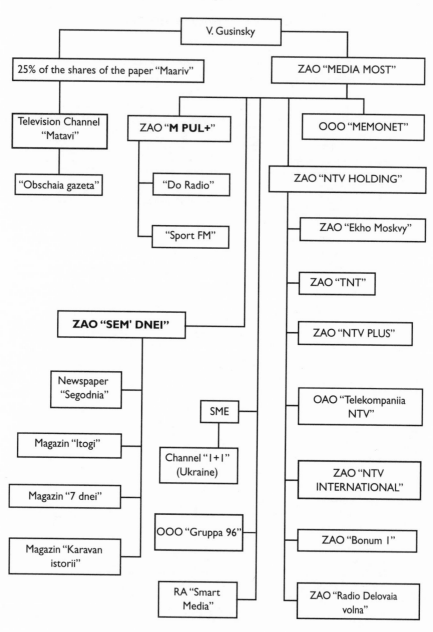

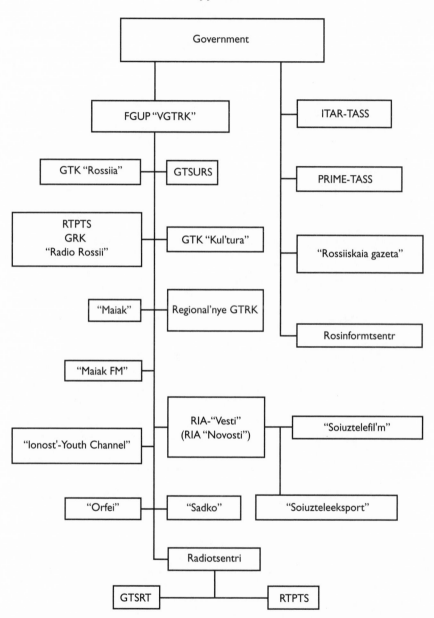

Chapter 2

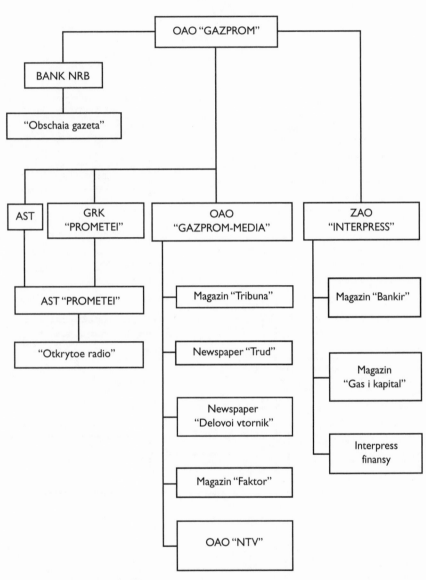

Source: *Izvestiia Media,* March 26, 2001.

3

Communications Technology

Globalization is often associated with other social processes, such as modernization or postindustrialization (Waters 1995, 4); thus, globalization is often connected with the latest communications technology. For example, Tomlinson defines globalization as "complex connectivity," referring to the rapidly developing and ever-expanding network of interconnections and interdependencies that characterize modern social life (1999, 2). Obviously, global connectivity is often mediated by information technology. As a consequence of the marriage between postindustrialization and globalization, each new form of technology, be it mobile phones or the Internet, is forecast to intensify the experience of globalization (see, for example Castells 1998). The effects of globalization are often equated simply with numbers—the more new communications technology one country has per inhabitant, the more globalized it is. The formula makes developing countries, and most postcommunist countries, losers in the globalization race.

Authors such as S. Frederick Starr (1984), Scott Shane (1994), Gladys Ganley (1996), and Loren R. Graham (1996) have already paid attention to the crucial role of information technology in the downfall of Communism. However, as this chapter will show, by supplementing previous analyses, in Russia it was globalization—with the help of communications technology and its social use—that challenged the old Communist system and now plays an important role in the restructuring of the new system. As a result, the role of

43

communications technology—in a country where the Iron Curtain, and, in effect, a media and communications curtain, has limited its citizens' exposure to the global network society for more than six decades—is now changing rapidly.

To analyze the role of new communications technology (NCT) in the process of globalization in Russia, we need to redefine the concept of NCT. Much of the research on NCT has concentrated on advanced Western countries. As a result, the definition of NCT is associated with the latest, most advanced technology. For example, Ronald Rice defines new media as "new" to the extent that they combine (1) computing, (2) telecommunications networks, and (3) digitization of content (1999, 24–25). In the case of Russia, the old and the new differ from their Western definitions. Set against the Western definitions of new—the latest technology and how widely it has been accepted—Russia's communications technology is mainly old and not widely used. Nevertheless, communication technologies have had profound effects on life in Russia. The change has taken place not from above but from below, because of the decrepit state of the Russian communications technology infrastructure.

The reasons for the underdevelopment of NCT derive from the past. In the Soviet Union, the telecommunications sector suffered from serious under-investment. Brian Regli has pointed to several factors that discouraged Soviet investment in the telecommunications sector (1997, 192). First, the Soviets had an aversion to "light," as opposed to "heavy," industries. An industry such as telecommunications, with a far less tangible output than iron, steel, or cement, was starved of funds and grew very slowly. Soviet authorities' statistics were unrelated to the true value of goods, so the potential value of communications services to the national economy went unrecognized. Second, statistics were distorted. Indicators such as kilometers of cable laid, or the number of apartments wired for telephone service, were calculated regardless of whether the apartment dwellers actually received telephone service. Third, official policy favored public access to telephones (telephone booths, central telegraph, and telephone stations) instead of private access. Prices (if connections worked) were kept artificially low, depriving telecommunications providers of requisite revenues for reinvestment. All of this information was only revealed after the collapse of Communism.

As a result, in present-day Russia, all evidence confirms that the availability of NCT is far behind that in the Western developed countries. In Russia in 1996, the number of main telephone lines per one hundred inhabitants was 16.86, and thirty-eight lines per one hundred households. The waiting time for telephone lines was ten years. Only 20 percent of the main telephone lines were digital. There were 0.15 cellular mobile phone subscribers per one hundred inhabitants. The number of personal computers per one hundred inhabitants was 2.37. Only 600,000 people of a population of 147.7 million used the Internet (*World Telecommunication Development Report* 1998).

A NEW APPROACH

Using a Western definition of NCT, Russia is a technologically backward country and thus unable to globalize itself. However, a reexamination of the old and new communications systems from a non-Western perspective reveals a technological environment that is rich in the variety of uses made available with communications tools, although that environment is very different from standard Western scenarios. In post-Communist Russia, the media system consists of the old and the new communications technology, which means that there are parts that originate from Imperial Russia (such as the telegraph and the telephone), and from the Soviet period (such as television). Sonia Livingstone makes a useful distinction between "technologically new" and "socially new" media. She writes: "The history of technological failures in this century alone demonstrates that which media succeed in dominating the market (and, as a result, everyday life) depends more on their *social shaping and contexts of use* than their technological capacities per se" (emphasis mine; Livingstone 1999, 59–60). Her distinction is useful in two different ways—to analyze new media and to examine the old and the new media in terms of their social use. I have combined technologically and socially new/old communication technology in a Russian context. As Table 3.1 illustrates, this model acknowledges the difference between media and communications technology and their social use. Technology—and how people use that technology—opens the door to globalization.

The first distinction, the technologically and socially new, takes place wherever NCT is introduced for the first time. In Russia, the

Table 3.1   Technologically and Socially New/Old Communication Technology in the Soviet Union/Russia

	Socially New	Socially Old
Technologically New	Internet Mobile phones	*Samizdat* Videos
Technologically Old	Telephone	Television

Internet or mobile phones would be examples. The second situation, the technologically old but socially new, occurs when technology has been available, but has not been widely used. The telephone in Russia would be an excellent example of this situation. The third combination, technologically and socially old, takes place when NCT has been introduced and accepted on a large scale. Russian television provides a case where it has become old in the sense that it has become a part of people's daily life. The fourth combination, technologically new but socially old, occurred in the Soviet Union when NCT (such as audiocassettes or video players) was not available to a larger audience, but the audience itself found ways to get access to it, mainly through foreign contacts. This was true with almost any NCT in the Soviet period and still partly continues to be so.

Following Livingstone's distinction between technologically and socially new, I consider it important to make another distinction—between big and small communications technology (see Sreberny-Mohammadi and Mohammadi 1994; Ganley 1996). While the state or military in the Soviet Union traditionally controlled big technology (such as telecommunications or the printing press), small technology (such as tapes, faxes, audiovisual cassettes, e-mail, etc.) was, to a certain extent, left outside state control. Some authors (for example, Ganley 1996) suggest that it was only during the last years before the USSR's collapse that control was noticeably relaxed, while others (for example, Starr 1984 and Graham 1998) give evidence of prior relaxation. This chapter will also suggest that small media could not be totally controlled, even in the Soviet period.

The division between big and small follows Elémer Hankiss's division (quoted in Goban-Klas 1994, 18) between the first and the second society in Communist countries. While the first society (official, approved, social life) used big technology, the second society (unofficial, often illegal, behavior) used small technology. The use of small technology matched the characteristics of the second society, which valued family and personal ties over purely formal relationships and rejected abstract and rigid organizations and rules (McDaniel 1996, 123–24). New technology was often first used by the second society but on a small scale.

A third important distinction, between centralized and decentralized communications technology, adds another dimension to that between big and small: control. While big, and often old, technology was controlled by the state (television, for example), the use of small and new technologies operated outside its control (videocassettes) in the Soviet Union. Also, centralized communications technology is often old (the telephone), while decentralized communications technology is new (mobile phones).

A fourth distinction is between foreign and domestic technology. In most cases, old, big, and centralized technology in Russia is domestic, while small, new, and decentralized technology is foreign in origin. Because foreign communications technology played a significant role in the collapse of the Soviet Union, questions of globalization and media imperialism are raised when its use is considered in post-Communist Russia.

In this chapter, I concentrate on the two combinations of technologically old but socially new, and technologically new but socially old, because they and their interrelationship help to explain the process of globalization and the dynamics of change in Russian society. This interplay also exemplifies the difference between Western and non-Western media and communications. Western communication scholarship has largely focused on the role of the media in creating mass society; the Russian perspective follows a different intellectual agenda that sees the role of the media as one which breaks down mass society and creates small communities.

COMMUNICATIONS TECHNOLOGY IN THE SOVIET UNION

It has been claimed that the first political casualty of the information age was the Communist state system, a system based on a 1920s model of hierarchical, industrial organization, incapable of incorporating new, flexible management or rapidly changing technology (Carnoy et al. 1993, 2). The most important factor that prevented the large-scale use of NCT was that the Soviet Union, despite its superpower status, was far behind the Western industrialized countries in the field of information technology and the industries arising from its application. This is surprising since, as an industrial power, its achievements were sometimes comparable even to those of the United States. Zygmund Bauman claims that Communism represented the final project of modernization (and took it more seriously than the West) by mobilizing and developing all of its social and natural resources (1992, 169). The statistics confirm this view. In the 1980s, for example, the Soviet Union produced substantially more than the United States in a number of heavy industrial sectors: 80 percent more steel, 78 percent more cement, 42 percent more oil, 55 percent more fertilizer, twice as much pig iron, and five times as many tractors (Castells 1998, 26, 27). The problem, according to Castells, was that the world's production system had shifted toward electronics and chemicals, areas in which the USSR lagged behind the United States. But above all, there was a profound disparity between the Soviet Union and the West in telecommunications and information technology. The information revolution that had started to change the structure of the advanced Western economies hardly touched the Soviet Union.

Although comprehensive statistics from the Soviet period are not available, the country lagged behind in new communications technology despite the fact that it was the world's third largest economy, with the world's largest community of scientists and engineers—exceeding that in the United States by 10 to 39 percent, depending on the definition of degrees and fields (Graham 1998, x). Significant resources in communication technology, particularly from the military-industrial sector, did in fact exist. As Graham writes, the history of computers in the Soviet Union is a graphic example of the failure of that country to blaze an independent path (1998, 39). In 1987, telecommunications equipment expenditures in the USSR amounted to $9.8 billion. Among industrialized countries, this represented less than half of projected U.S. spending ($24.3 billion). Comparable figures for Soviet computers and related equipment are even more difficult to obtain, even though the USSR was a major producer of such equipment, particularly larger machines (Dizard and Swensrud

1987, 2–4). Again, the Soviet Union was more successful in producing big (hardware) rather than small (software) technology (Downing 1989a, 111–12).

According to Seymour Goodman, a "Soviet-style information society" was characterized by goals rather than trends (1998, 13–14). He lists four primary goals of this information society:

- to attain real gains in productivity and to modernize the industrial base;
- to improve the economic planning and control mechanism;
- to support both military and internal security needs;
- to present the image of a progressive society both to the people of the USSR and to the outside world.

Compared with the West, where according to Goodman, driving forces were opportunities for innovations, large and diversified push-pull markets, and fierce domestic and international competition, driving forces in the Soviet Union were national-level political processes and Western achievements (1998, 15). The major problem was that for over sixty years, as Wilson Dizard and S. Blake Swensrud point out, the limited Soviet resources were committed to the party's control mechanisms (1997, 8). According to Castells, Soviet statism denied itself the diffusion of information technologies throughout the social system (1998, 36). He writes:

> Thus, at the core of the technological crisis of the Soviet Union, lies the fundamental logic of the statist system: overwhelming priority given to military power; political-ideological control of information by the state; the bureaucratic principle of the centrally planned economy; isolation from the rest of the world; and an inability to modernize some segments of the economy and society technologically, without modifying the whole system in which such elements interact with each other.

The policy adopted meant that society at large could not use the means of communications properly. Use of computers that were installed in workplaces in the late 1950s and 1960s was controlled (Dizard and Swensrud 1987, 27–29). Telephones were available primarily to organizations. In the first half of the 1980s, the USSR had about 28 million phones; the United States, with about the same population, had 170 million phones. Soviets made 2 billion intercity calls a year; Americans made 45 billion (Ganley 1996, 17). Government policy favored public telephones for individual use. Every visitor to Moscow or Leningrad during the Communist period remembers the main telegraph and telephone station, where you had to order your intercity or foreign call sometimes even days ahead, without knowing whether you would actually get through at the appointed time.

The social use of the telephone was not only technically difficult, but also heavily controlled. The state control of telephoning, begun in Imperial Russia, also influenced the structure of the system. The Soviet telephone system was vertically organized—instead of having several hubs, all calls came through Moscow—a system that gave authorities the opportunity to monitor citizens and visitors (Dizard and Swensrud 1987, 29). This, in turn, drove people to use public telephones, which were considered more difficult to monitor.

The Social Use of Communications

The difference between the uses of new technology in the Communist period from that in the West was that the flow between technologically new and socially new was not straightforward. In the advanced Western countries, the main obstacle to the social use of NCT is its affordability. The latest technology is available to consumers who can pay the asking price. In contrast, in the Soviet Union, NCT was used exclusively for state and military purposes, was not manufactured for mass markets, and did not necessarily become widely socially used. If it did reach the market (and always with a considerable delay), citizens gained access to it after long delays, or by buying it abroad or on the black market. As a result, there was a long hiatus between technologically new communications and socially new communications. People who first had access to technologically new communications had either high social status (but not necessarily wealth) within the Communist Party, or foreign contacts. In the latter case, people associated NCT with access to the West and it became identified with restricted access to globalization.

When NCT was connected with access to the West, it started to exist almost independently of Communist state structures, despite attempts to restrict and control it. Its liberating role was an additional factor in the social adoption of NCT as Starr (1984), Shane (1994), Ganley (1996), and Graham (1998) have shown. Again, I would add that it was not only new technology that played a decisive role in the collapse of Communism, bearing in mind that that the old and the new have different meanings in communist countries, but that communication technology was also an agent of globalization. As Slavko Splichal argues, the democratic revolutions in Central and Eastern Europe might not have succeeded without the globalization of the communication sphere (1994, 23). Raymond Pearson writes about the availability of technology in the Soviet Union:

> The growing availability of typewriters and tape recorders, then photocopiers (against which the KGB had battled for years), and finally word processors made alternative information dissemination unstoppable. The collective impact of the 1980s' revolution in media technology made the traditional Soviet insistence on its hermetic monopoly of news through the exercise of information suppression and diffusion problematic to the point of being almost quaintly anachronistic. (1998, 114–15)

Most NCT was foreign, either imported illegally or broadcast from abroad. Because it was imported from abroad, the question of globalization cannot be ignored. The globalizing elements in Soviet society were mainly imported through communications. If globalization is defined as connectivity (Tomlinson 1999, 2), the liberating aspect of NCT in the Communist era becomes more visible. With the help of NCT, ordinary citizens could connect themselves to the outside world, mainly the West. This is an aspect of globalization with which some theorists feel uneasy. The first wave of globalization theorists saw the process mainly as a form of Western media imperialism, and thus found it difficult to acknowledge an alternative, liberating role. The Soviet Union did everything it could to protect its citizens against Western influence, but communications technology made its presence unstoppable. These sentiments are expressed in the statement of Lennart Meri, at that time the Estonian Foreign Minister, and later, President, when he proposed in *Izvestiia* in 1991 that the Radio Free Europe/Radio Liberty be a candidate for the Nobel Peace Prize "for its unique contribution to the revival of democracy in our region and throughout the world" (quoted in Manaev 1991, 89).

The boundaries that were once considered impermeable became permeable, largely because of NCT and its new social use in the communist countries. There are several examples of how old and new communications technology were used for connections beyond state and party control. Although the printing press is socially and technologically old, it acquired a new social use in the underground press. As Tomasz Goban-Klas has observed, underground (*samizdat)* publications became virtually a second literary system in Eastern Europe, overcoming governmental control of the printing press (1994, 156). The entire *samizdat* movement resembled the cultural environment in Europe before the invention of printing (Feldbrugge 1975, 18). *Samizdat* publication (self-publishing house) meant typed, single-spaced sheets, without margins, often on blurry carbon copies distributed by hand (Feldbrugge 1975, 18; Downing 1996, 74). But electronic communication went a step farther: The term *radiszdat* was sometimes used for transcription of foreign radio broadcasts, *magnizdat,* or *magnitizdat,* referred to taped copies of *samizdat* or *radizdat* items and to circulated Russian guitar-poetry and pirated Western rock music. Finally, with the arrival of the videocassette, this process expanded still farther: *tamizdat* media ("tam" translates to "there" in Russian), published in the West and smuggled back in, consisted initially of print, and later of electronic media (Feldbrugge 1975, 4; Downing 1996, 75).

The Soviet authorities tried to prevent foreign visitors from bringing in their typewriters or magazines, but broadcasting crossed Soviet borders more effortlessly because it did not need a carrier other than air. Broadcasting has never respected the national boundaries of maps. It was a technologically and socially old form of media, but Western radio stations broadcasting anti-Communist programs created a new social use of radio in the Soviet Union. The Soviet listeners tuned into the Western stations to listen to music, news, and literature that were censored. For example, Radio Free Europe broadcast readings of Solzhenitsyn's *Gulag Archipelago* (Nelson 1998, 149), a banned book in the Soviet Union, thus combining written, oral, and electronic communication.

Western radio stations drew large audiences, thus challenging the dominant position of state-controlled broadcasting. Western stations never threatened state-controlled broadcasting's position, but became an alternative, especially in the times of domestic or international crises. For example, in 1984, the Voice of America reached 14 to 18 percent of the adult population, Radio Liberty 8 to 12 percent, the BBC reached 7 to 10 percent and *Deutsche Welle* 3 to 6 percent. On the other hand, in Belarus in 1985, 63 percent of young people between the ages of sixteen and thirty listened to Western radio. Two years later the total number of listeners in this age group exceeded 83 percent (Manaev 1991, 73; Nelson 1998, 163). The authorities' attempts to control communications technology became more difficult with the rapid development of NCT. Their efforts to jam Western radio stations' programs were only partly successful, and they proved to be very expensive. In 1971, it was estimated that jamming operations cost the Soviet Union $300 million (Ellis 1998, 209). In 1981, the BBC estimated that just four days of jamming cost the Soviet Union as much as the BBC's Russian service cost for a whole year (Nelson 1998, 24). In addition, people increasingly watched television broadcasts from neighboring countries. Estonians watched Finnish television to the extent that Finnish was fluently and widely spoken in Estonia. Through Finnish advertisements, Estonians learned about the standard of living in Finland.

Again, the definitions and social uses of NCT were different from those of the advanced Western countries. Young people listened mostly to Western music from foreign broadcasts. In Belarus, nearly three-quarters of young people listening to Western radio preferred music to other types of programming (Manaev 1991, 73). If Western pop music was not available in shops, copies were made privately and then distributed from hand to hand (see, for example, Troitsky 1987, 83–86). Until the 1960s, young people made so-called X-ray plates, or rib records, using X-ray pictures to record music and then cut them into the form of a record. This was called *roentgenizdat*, again, a new form of people's technology that preceded *magnizdat*, or cassette copying (Ryback 1990, 32, 44; Helin 1999, 34). Gradually, with the development of technology, copying records and music cassettes became a business, and cassettes were eventually sold. In 1990, the state-owned music company, *Melodia*, finally decided to release an album by the extremely popular Soviet rock group Nautilus-Pampilus; by that time, most of the group's songs from 1985–1987 were already known to the audience (Orlova 1991, 68). Of course, if the records had been available, the new social use would not have begun and been developed. When mass-produced and mass-distributed cassettes became widely available, the cassettes were already socially old.

If the mail and the telephone networks did not have wide reaches, and if the authorities did not favor their use by individuals, television, on the other hand, was almost ubiquitous. Over 80 percent of households owned television sets. The official policy favored the rapid expansion of television, because it was easy to control. Satellites sent the programs from Moscow to different Soviet republics. The contents of the programs were to a certain extent educational, although Soviet audiences had always enjoyed watching films. Most of the films were domestically produced, and few foreign films were shown.

The wide social use of television created a market for VCRs and videocassettes. Almost every household had a television, but there was little space for individual choice of programs. The old television created the new video, because the old could not provide the viewers with the content they wanted. The television set was essential for using video and became a necessary launching base for new technology. This is again one of the examples of how the old and the new were combined. Video was new technology, but the Soviet video industry was slow to respond to the demand. Prices were also high— the state price of a Soviet VCR was 1,200 rubles in 1988; the street price of a foreign VCR was around 5,000 rubles, equivalent to a substantial annual salary (Shane 1994, 204). VCRs, as other forms of NCT, were increasingly imported, using the networks of the second society. Shane describes how this took place:

> As travel restrictions eased beginning in 1987, many people fortunate enough to be able to travel to the United States or Western Europe scraped together a few hundred dollars from friends or relatives abroad in order to buy a VCR, boom box, computer, or fax machine to bring back and sell. . . . VCRs and other consumer electronics, like many other imported items, also entered the country with truck drivers on European runs and sailors returning from Asian voyages. Another source was barter deals: a steel plant, for instance, would rather trade a few tons of steel plate for a shipment of VCRs or other hard-to-get items, which would then be sold to employees for modest ruble price. (1994, 204–5)

The social use of VCRs had wider consequences. Dona Kolar-Panov has noted how the capacity of new media technologies, such as VCRs, joins the private sphere of home and family with the larger public realms beyond the boundary of the front door. It allows people to be in touch with places that are distant in time and space, and creates symbolic communities that in turn have offered identification points to audience members of a transnational character (1997, 23). In the Soviet Union, videocassettes provided private access to Western mass culture that public policy prohibited.

Despite the authorities' efforts, the Communist era audio- and videocassettes provided people with access to Western popular culture. If the government-controlled television did not show a film, it was often available on a videocassette on the black market. The same was true for Western pop music. Blank video- and audiocassettes were sometimes hard to find, but were available in *beriozhka* shops, special state-owned shops for tourists where only foreigners could buy goods, only with foreign currency. Copying was free, because the market officially did not exist. As a result, the Soviet Union, and, later, Russia, became one of the leading countries in pirating. The International Intellectual Property Alliance estimated that intellectual property rights violations in twenty-three problem countries (including Russia) against American film and video programming accounted for at least $1.02 billion in lost revenue ("Globalization of the Mass Media" 1993, 98).

Hence, in the late years of the Communist era, NCT was present in three Soviet markets. There was advanced high technology (computers and satellites) available only to a restricted number of people for security and military reasons. The big technology of television and telecommunications did not work very well, but it was cheap and available to citizens in various forms (television sets at home and public telephones). There was also the people's market, in which *samizdat* material and video and music cassettes were exchanged either for services, other products, or money. While big technology was mainly produced at home, the small technology was mainly imported from the West. These three markets converged when Communism collapsed.

The Old Meets the New

When the Soviet control systems started to loosen, what was earlier forbidden became tolerated, if not officially accepted. What had previously been done secretly in the second, private society became more visible and open. This process took place simultaneously with the commercialization of media, as the first private media firms were established in the late 1980s and early 1990s (Rantanen and Vartanova 1995, 210). NCT that was earlier used by people in the second society for mainly private purposes was now needed for establishing new enterprises. A new commercial social use was born in the mass market. The boundaries between the first and the second societies began to fade.

By early 1990, there were still only a few thousand fax machines in the Soviet Union (Ganley 1996, 23). The interaction between the old and the new, the big and the small, and the foreign and the domestic was explained by Mikhail Komissar, one of the founders of the first private news agencies, Interfax, in an interview in which he described the beginnings of the new agency in 1989:

> In those years, nobody knew about telecommunications and computers. We didn't have money. Suddenly I found a chapter in a popular magazine, *Nauka i Zhizn* (Science and Life), about telefax. I knew some foreigners on the basis of my contacts, but only a few of them had telefaxes. I spent $30,000 to rent computers and telefaxes from a firm, Interquadro, and abroad. We were the first to rent them in this country. In two months we had one hundred clients, mainly Japanese journalists.

Komissar's description shows the leaks in a system that was considered waterproof. There are several aspects of Komissar's statement that explain Interfax's success. First, individuals played an important pioneering role in adopting new technology. Second, foreign contacts and financial support were crucial in getting access to new technology. And third, good working relations with the authorities were also essential. Interfax was born within an existing state-owned organization, *Gosteleradio* (the State Committee for Television and Radio Broadcasting), and was able to use the latter's infrastructure (telephone lines) to support the new technology. Even after it became an independent organization, Interfax was able to use the contacts it had with the authorities to guarantee access to NCT.

On the other hand, although most firms started using small technology, they later also needed big technology. This was a crucial point for the transition period. The interests of the first and second societies moved closer to each other. The first society's control over the second society loosened, and made their mutual cooperation possible. The second society needed the first society to provide infrastructure, while the first society needed the second society for developing the new market economy. The second society was more experienced than the first in the market economy, albeit on a small scale. However, the two societies traveled at different speeds, and the pace of change in the second society was too fast for the first society. The first society could not provide the technology that was vital for the large-scale use of NCTs. The state's inability was clearly visible in four key areas: (1) technology, (2) finance, (3) legislation, and (4) national security.

First, the existing networks could not provide the platform on which modern communications networks, such as the Internet, are built. For example, since the introduction of the telephone, twisted copper wires, often fifty years old, rather than fiber or wireless networks, had made up the local loop (Davies et al. 1996, 101, 106). In all major aspects—extensiveness, ability to interconnect, level of technology used, and quality—the Russian telecommunications system inherited from the Soviet period was backward. Most importantly, the general telephone network in the former Soviet Union could not support data communications at any appreciable speeds (McHenry 1988, 87). The state could not produce the services that were needed to change the structure of the new economy. Many foreign companies brought in their own technology after import restrictions were lifted. Foreign media companies like Reuters furnished their own satellite dishes because they either could not, or would not, rely on the old Soviet technology. Even new Russian enterprises had to turn to foreign companies to get access to the modern technology they required.

Second, the replacement of old technology was, of course, primarily a question of money, for the state-owned telecommunications sector had, throughout its existence, suffered from a lack of funding. Unlike many telecommunications companies in Central and Eastern Europe, the privatization of the national telecommunications company did not attract a substantial amount of foreign investment to the sector. Instead, foreign companies bought shares in local companies, mainly in big cities. One of the first to do so was Sprint (subsequently bought by Global One) in 1991. Global One Russia, as the company is now called, is a joint venture between Moscow Central Telegraph (40 percent) and Global One (60 percent). However, its primary clientele is not people, but banks and business—nearly 70 percent of the traffic originates from Russian enterprises. AT&T also formed a joint stock company in Moscow with the Moscow City Telephone Company in 1993 ("Diversity and Disarray" 1997, 30).

A private telecommunications company, Finnet, which provides a quarter of Finland's international telephone traffic market, provides another example of how NCT has been introduced into Russia by foreign companies. Finnet International has constructed, procured, or leased fiber-optic or other similar capacities on three cables from Helsinki—via Copenhagen, Tallinn, or Lappenranta—to St. Petersburg, with various Russian counterparts owning the Russian parts of the circuits and further links to other parts of the country (Mårtenson 1998).

Comprehensive legislation regulating new communication technologies lags behind the actual changes. Instead, discrete, often contradictory, laws are in place. Russia has no telecommunications law per se. Computing in Russia is regulated by several pieces of primary legislation, in addition to the provisions of the 1992 Mass Media Law and its amendments (Ellis 1998, 149–50).

The issues of national security and protection of the state are inseparable from the development of NCT in Russia (Meliukhin 1997, 195; Vartanova 1998b, 186). The state wants to maintain its grip over NCT because it fears that its widespread popular use may have a negative impact on national security. As Frank Ellis points out (1999, 157), Chapter 14 of the Law on Information Exchange potentially represents a major threat to online free speech in present-day Russia in the following provisions:

1. the dissemination of unreliable, false foreign documentary information, received as a result of international exchange, on the territory of the Russian Federation is not permitted;
2. responsibility for the dissemination of such information falls on the legal subject of the international information exchange, who has received such information and (or) disseminates it on the territory of the Russian Federation.

Zassoursky and Vartanova (1999) have listed further reasons for the slow development of NCT in Russia. They are:

- increasing depression in the Russian economy and low income level;
- technical incompatibility of international and Russian networks;
- high prices for the use of international communications channels;
- still-existing monopoly of the Ministry of Communications;
- internal organization of the Internet and its relations with the state;
- underdeveloped infrastructure for the use of credit cards, electronic mail, electronic shopping, alternative delivery service, etc.

The introduction of NCT into wider use has been slow in Russia compared to Western countries because it is constrained by established state structures. Although NCT provides new opportunities for individuals, old technology and structures set boundaries to the growth of new technology.

The New Social Uses of Communications

If new businesses in Russia were successful in gaining access to NCT, often with the help of foreign companies, ordinary citizens were not. NCT was introduced first to serve the interests of banks and businesses. For example, the telecommunications infrastructure can be subdivided in two parts—an old copper post, telegraph, and telephone network for citizens, and modern fiber-based digital technology for enterprises (Denisov 1996, 10). Most Russian citizens cannot afford the private service that is now available to them. Mobile phone rates, for example, are not affordable by ordinary people.

In worsening economic circumstances, many Russians could not afford to have a telephone installed at home. Many people still use public phones as in the Soviet era. The Starodubov family's social use of the telephone is not exceptional:

Mr. Starodubov, looking since May for his salary from Baikonur, picks up his umbrella and goes outside to a pay phone. The Starodubovs don't have a phone in their apartment, while the service itself is cheap, installing a phone means either waiting at least five years for the state to allocate a line, or paying around 2,000 dollars for a private service. (McKay 1998)

When the market system started to develop, people's private access to communication technology became increasingly a question of money. This was difficult for Russians, who were not used to paying more than a nominal sum for their telephone calls. As Cathy Bryan et al. note, citizens' rights in the era of telecommunications and public service broadcasting are easily replaced with consumer rights (1998, 3). This is, of course, exactly what happened in Russia when the market economy expanded at a very rapid pace, almost without warning.

The majority of new Russian consumers had little income when prices skyrocketed after the "liberalization" of the market. At the end of 1991, 15 percent of the population in Russia lived below the poverty level; by the spring of 1993, it had risen to 60 percent of the population. In this situation, many people could not afford to communicate by either mail or phone. In the spring of 1992, the lowest monthly salary was equivalent to the cost of a 10-minute telephone call from Moscow to New York, and it would have cost two months' wages to send an express mail letter to the United States (Androunas 1993, 120). As a result, as Vartanova has observed, information inequality became the most visible result of the new market economy (1998a, 177).

In the Russian case, the social uses of NCT again differed from those of the advanced Western countries. For example, it is essential to have a working telephone network in order to use electronic mail. If the old technology is not working, or access is patchy (as is the case with Russian telephone lines), then the growth of the new technology is strictly limited. But some Russians managed to access E-mail technology through their own combination of the old and the new. The faculty of journalism at Moscow University provides an illuminating example of how the old and new were combined before 1998—when there was only one computer that was able to receive electronic mail, the messages were printed out and delivered to staff members by hand. The adaptation of the Western experience of private and fast

E-mail to the reality of the Russian university context nevertheless provided an opportunity for staff to be connected with foreign scholars at a time when the telephone worked unreliably and foreign calls were expensive.

Video is still a new technology to most people in Russia. Much of its success can be explained by the fact that television is widely available, unlike telephone networks. Thus, it is possible for the new to combine with the old. In 1988, 0.9 percent of the households with televisions had videocassette recorders (*World Communication Report* 1989, 159). In 1994, every tenth Russian household had a video recorder. In 1996, VCR distribution in European Russia already stood at 27 percent (Lutz and Jankowski 1998, 78). Of course, the figures are still low compared to more technologically advanced countries. In the West, the first videocassette recorders were introduced in 1965 (Kolar-Panov 1997, 14). In Australia, by the late 1980s, video ownership in households with televisions was over 78 percent. The country with the highest usage is Kuwait, with 85.5 percent penetration, while in the United States it is 71.5 percent, in Canada, 70 percent, and in the U.K., 71.5 percent (Kolar-Panov 1997, 16).

Although a new copyright law was introduced in 1995, pirated copies still dominate the market. Illegally copied video and music cassettes are mainly distributed outside the official market and sold in local kiosks. According to Gladys Ganley, from at least the early 1980s, all manner of Western programming was regularly taped from Finnish television by Estonians, and sold around the USSR (1996, 78). As a result of increased taping, the most preferred contemporary American films on tape in the Soviet Union in 1983 included *The Deer Hunter, One Flew Over the Cuckoo's Nest,* and *Last Tango in Paris* (Boyd 1989, 259). By 1990, when it became legal for individuals to import or buy satellite dishes and antennas, pirated tapings from them increased the supply of foreign programs considerably (Ganley 1996, 78). In contrast to the Soviet period, several Russian television channels now provide viewers with films that were earlier available only on pirated cassettes. As a result, the gap between what has been accessible through television and through video has been narrowed.

CONCLUSION

A very different picture of the production and consumption of NCT from those studies conducted in Western countries emerges from an examination of the conditions in post-Communist Russia, a country often considered "the Other" by Western scholars, and thus often neglected by them. As a result, most theories that are considered to have universal validity are actually based on empirical data gathered only in advanced Western countries. This is especially true when we talk about the theories of globalization that so often refer to advanced media and communications technology. The Russian case study shows that it is not only the availability of the latest new communications technology but also its social use of the latest communications technology that plays a decisive role in globalization.

The Russian case study also shows that globalization does take place in closed societies, such as in Communist Russia, where, by Western standards, only scarce and old technology was available. As I have shown in this chapter, globalization first reached the second society through small, informal, and often illegal communications technology, through its innovative social use (often collective), rather than mass-scale technological availability and individual use. In the Soviet Union, small and imported technology was used to spread messages that were suppressed or ignored by big government-owned and controlled media. The relationship between the technologically new and the socially new is not straightforward in Russia, and it requires a more subtle analysis and appreciation from scholars. The old and the new technologies are interwoven, both in their production and in their consumption.

An important factor is the cross-reaction between the old and the new media and communications, which covers many aspects including technology, contents, and social use. Old television and new video, for example, are connected to each other. Earlier, there was only Soviet television and it did not meet the expectations of its entire audience—Soviet television showed only domestically produced programs that lacked the features of many Western movies and serials. These features came to symbolize freedom and individual choice that were missing in Soviet society because of denied access to the outside (non-Communist) world. Soviet audiences found their way to these programs through individual use of videocassettes—again, items that became an object of desire. Although there was no mass market in the second society, there was widespread social use of the small media of video- and tape recorders. After the collapse of the Communist system, when both old and new Russian television stations started to show Western films, the old and the new converged through their similar (new) contents.

There are also examples of disconnectivity. Television, videos, and advertising are connected to each other, because both the technology and contents support each other. Telephone, fax, and E-mail, on the other hand, are not, because there is no shared content. The old technology was poor, but needed, to build the new. Fax and E-mail need a working telephone net, something that did not exist in Russia. Unlike television, which was available to almost everybody, the telephone was not widely available. After the system collapsed, new technology could not be properly introduced because old technology did not meet the standards the implementation of new technology demanded.

Disconnectivity is not only an issue of technology but of adopted policy. John Downing outlines two democratic modes of democratic communication, the Western (Tocquevillean) and the Eastern (Leninist) mode (1989b, 156). While the first is based on loose local associations, the second mode confronts a strong, centralized state with its own weapons. Neither of them is sufficient as such, but Downing sees a future in their combination:

> In a democratic telecommunications network, or in the relations between data processing service institutes and their clients, there are multiple centers of the production of information offering the pool their resources. This suggests the kernel of an alternative model of democratic communication, one that enjoys some of the advantages of the Tocquevillean and Leninist models without suffering from their dysfunctions. The technology itself, of course, cannot make such differences operational, but the[se] examples of its use and of its potential for being simultaneously decentred and coordinating, may combine to illustrate the scope for new modes of political communication. (1989b, 156–57)

In post-Communist Russia, Eastern and Western models met each other. The second society's multiple centers worked well when they opposed the dominant system, but after the collapse of Communism, they did not take over the dominant system that was based on centralized, state-controlled communications technology. Although new and small technologies play an important role in creating new social structures, it is important to remember that they never operate in a social vacuum. This helps us to understand why the transition from Communism to post-Communism is not an easy one in a society that is going through fundamental changes, but which at the same time has inherited some rigid structures and state control from the past. The restratification of first and second societies that I have described is both the cause and the consequence of the introduction of NCT in Russia, and these social factors, of course, shape, and are shaped by, specifically communicational factors.

A further difference lies in that between domestic and foreign technology, which again raises the issue of globalization, and of Westernization. In the Soviet period, NCT was seen as mainly Western, despite the availability of cassette recorders and VCRs that were probably of Asian origin. It was the technologically advanced West that became the promised land of NCT for Russia. The standard was Western, and one the Soviet Union never reached, despite the claims of official ideology and propaganda. This attitude was inherited from the Soviet period, and has proved very difficult to change. It has been strengthened by the fact that the Russian state could not immediately react to new demands for NCT, and had to import the latest technology from abroad. Thus, Western technology, at first a sign of liberation and resistance, became a status symbol in the new market economy of Russia.

4

News Agencies

News agencies were, and partly still are, key institutions in any media system—the nerve center that connects all its parts, be it electronic or print medium, big or small, capital or provincial. But news agencies are also in their own class compared to other forms of media and communications. News agencies are neither media nor communications, but they still share features that are typical of both. News agencies are media in the sense that they deliver their contents en masse, but they do not have an audience; like communications, news agencies often supply content to media, which then use that content to become mass media and reach their audience. A news agency's "audience" is other media that are actually the agency's clients and suppliers of news at the same time. Hence, people do not use news agencies socially. However, with the development of new communications technology, news agencies could deliver their contents directly to audiences (for example, through the Internet), but still not reach a mass audience in the same sense as traditional mass media (people consuming it in the same place at the same time).

Of all media institutions in present-day Russia, news agencies are the oldest, already in existence in the nineteenth century (Rantanen 1990). News agencies have survived the major political changes in Russia, from autocracy to Communism, and then from Communism to a transition period moving toward a state capitalist system. Hence, news agencies clearly represent "the old" compared to other media. The key characteristic of their development is that news agencies have always been very closely affiliated to the state, be it autocratic, communist, or the present transitional form.

We encounter here a paradox—Russian news agencies have long been affiliated with the state, while at the same time, they have also promoted globalization. Nineteenth-century news agencies were the first electronic media that significantly contributed to globalization by delivering messages from all parts of the world with the speed of electricity. Although the first Russian news agencies were founded at the same time as elsewhere in Europe, they soon came to represent the interests of the autocratic Russian state. News agencies had a double mission—on the one hand, they connected Russia with the rest of the world; on the other hand, they separated Russia from the rest of the world because of the interests of the autocratic state. This contradiction has always been clearly visible in Russia; of course, it also happens in other countries—including Western Europe— especially in periods of crisis, such as internal disturbances or wars.

This contradictory double mission is the reason why news agencies are interesting when we want to study the relationship between the global and the national. News agencies have contributed to both, often at the same time. It was (and still is, as we have seen in post-communist countries) important that every country should have its own news agency; even the names of the agencies—for example, the Russian Telegraph Agency, TASS—reflected this importance. News agencies were traditionally national institutions, and their task was to serve every kind of national media, from print to electronic, from large to small, from capital to provincial (Rantanen 1998, 125). As Oliver Boyd-Barrett has pointed out, news agencies also constructed the national by reinforcing the status of the nation's capital by elect- ing the capital as its hub, and as the "natural" center of news gath- ered throughout the territories governed by the nation-state (2000, 309). Again, the names of agencies underline this fact: many of them were named after the capital, such as the St. Petersburg Telegraph Agency, in the beginning of the 20th century.

However, because of their long history and because the media sys- tem around them is rapidly changing, national news agencies every- where seem now to be in crisis (Boyd-Barrett and Rantanen 2000). The crisis has been associated with national news agencies in general, but has been most visible in Central and Eastern Europe. Why is it, then, that state-owned news agencies are losing their former status in the postcommunist countries? Not only do ITAR-TASS (former TASS) and RIA-Novosti (former Novosti (APN)) in Russia have problems, but state-owned news agencies in Central and Eastern Europe are going through a similar kind of process. In part, they face difficulties because the status of almost all national news agencies is declining in the face of a new competitive media environment (see Boyd-Barrett and Rantanen 1998); furthermore, as news agencies in the communist countries, they had a special status compared to other media in their relationship to the state and the Communist parties. In the case of ITAR-TASS and RIA-Novosti, it is not only a question of a national news agency losing its privileged position in the home market but also of a global news agency losing out in the global market.

The dilemma of postcommunist news agencies lies in their uneasy position between the processes of globalization and nation building. National news agencies were among the institutions that new nation-states had to establish, both to be seen credible as nations and to project or control the dissemination of their "national image" on global markets (Boyd-Barrett and Rantanen 1998, 5). Their task was not only about constructing a national image, but also about protecting a national interest. In general, national interest in communications involves protecting a particular section of the market against foreign investors. However, in extreme cases, national interest may also involve control over the contents of information through censorship. This was the case in Imperial Russia, as well as in the Communist Soviet Union. The task of protecting the state's or the party's interests clashed with their role as news transmitters. There are numerous examples both from Imperial Russia and the Soviet Union, when news has either been delayed or censored because of the state's or the party's interests. This was made possible by having the headquarters of the agencies located in the capital, where the task to monitor in- and outgoing news was made easier by centralizing both the production and the distribution of news there.

Even if news censorship were not the central function of a present-day Russian news agency, it still serves the function of constructing a national image. In the postcommunist period, when a Soviet image is no longer appropriate, any agency is central to the construction of the new Russian image. Because TASS traditionally distributed the "correct" national image in the Soviet Union, it is easy to see why the new Russian state is reluctant to give up control of it and other news agencies. The problem is that it is difficult to promote a national image when it can only emerge within the structures inherited from the past, a past now repudiated by official and popular consensus. To know what is in the national interest during a period of political and economic transition is also difficult—foreign investment and foreign technology are often urgently needed. The opening of the market to foreign capital inevitably raises the question of global versus national markets, and global interests versus national interests.

This chapter examines the role of Russian state-owned news agencies in an increasingly globalized environment—their relationship with the state, with the market and with domestic and global competitors. It deals with the new economic and political situation state-owned news agencies face, one in which the powerlessness and insecurity of the government in its communication policy becomes very clear—it does not seem to know what to do with state-owned news agencies, except to keep them under its control. The government wants to maintain its grip on its news agencies, but is reluctant to make necessary radical changes to improve their position in the market.

FROM COMMUNISM TO CAPITALISM

In its day, the Soviet news agency TASS gave the impression that there was no other media institution closer to officialdom. Its status was considered almost equal to the Soviet government and the Communist Party, and its voice was the voice of these institutions, as the phrase "TASS is authorized to announce" exemplified. Other national agencies in the Communist bloc imitated TASS and were the organs of their respective governments and parties. The law protected their status—they had a monopoly in their home countries because only state-owned agencies were permitted to operate. They were the gatekeepers of in- and out-going news and were largely responsible for the image of their country abroad and the image of foreign countries at home.

Of course, TASS's official status had an influence on its organizational culture. The government appointed its general managers, and its foreign correspondents had a status equivalent to diplomats. Journalists' appointments were based not only on professional skills, but also equally on reliability and loyalty as party members. TASS was a huge organization compared to its Western counterparts. For example, in 1993, TASS had 5,000 employees, considerably more than either the U.S. Associated Press (AP) or the French Agence France-Presse (AFP) had (Rantanen and Vartanova 1995, 214). The same was true with state-owned agencies in Central and Eastern European (CEE) countries—in 1990 the Hungarian news agency MTI had 1,400 staff members, while the Czech agency had 1,100. TASS's correspondent network was extensive, covering countries around the world, including the developing nations. National agencies in Central and Eastern Europe also had correspondent networks that were much larger than their counterparts in Western Europe (Rantanen 1998, 131).

TASS's size and number of clients gave it the status of a global agency, as one of the "Big Five" agencies that dominated the world's news market. TASS was the communist equivalent of Reuters, AFP, Associated Press (AP), and United Press International (UPI), but had most of its clients in the communist countries. In this sense, it represented the Soviet Union's international image. It had almost the same status as the Western agencies—but not quite. The main difference was that it did not follow the same criteria for news selection, and produced a product different from, and unattractive to, Western media. According to several studies, news credited to TASS by Western media was minimal (at most 1 percent) and hardly ever cited in most noncommunist countries. Even in Eastern Europe its usage was low (Sreberny-Mohammadi et al. 1985, 51). Most of TASS's Western clients were communist newspapers that relied on it for political reasons, not for the standard commercial ones of competing with rivals for the latest news. Timeliness was not a news criterion for TASS or for other communist news agencies.

However, to a certain extent, Western noncommunist media did use TASS's news product. Denied the operational privileges in the Soviet Union as they had in the West, Western noncommunist media needed TASS's official news service. TASS's material was used as raw material that was then commented upon, read between the lines, and interpreted by Western journalists. In this sense, a national agency in a communist country was as important to global news distribution as national agencies in other countries, but because of the mistrust in its service, it was the Western commentary on TASS's news that received international distribution.

Even when Communism collapsed, TASS (later ITAR-TASS) maintained its role as a voice of the new government. Nevertheless, at the same time, it lost some of its former privileges, the most important of which was its monopoly in the domestic market. New private domestic agencies were established, and Western agencies could enter the market without ITAR-TASS's intermediary role. ITAR-TASS was still protected by the state, but was also partly stripped of its former status. The liberalization of the media market also meant that finding new sources of revenues became more difficult.

Many Russian media organizations started to change internally under the old Soviet regime. For example, broadcasting programs challenged the old prevailing system before it collapsed (Rantanen and Vartanova 1995, 210). However, there were no external signs that TASS had started to change before the system collapsed, as the organization was too moribund and too close to the center of power to be able to do so. Thus, TASS missed its decisive moment and change was imposed from outside, as shown, for example, in its keeping its old name.

In contrast to most Central and Eastern European countries, the Soviet Union, and later Russia, witnessed a boom in private agencies. One of the first private agencies to enter the market was Postfactum, which started in 1987 as a branch office of the information service, Fact. Two years later it was registered as Postfactum, an independent joint-stock company. Interfax, the private agency that became powerful enough to challenge the position of TASS, began to operate in 1989 (Rantanen and Vartanova 1995, 211–12).

The Legal Status of State-Owned Agencies

As usual in postcommunist countries, legislation was slow to follow the actual events that dismantled the old system. The Press Law was passed in 1990, but hardly touched news agencies ("O sredstvakh massovoi informatsii" 1996, 17). Article 23 of the Russian Mass Media Law of 1991 secured the status of all news agencies. According to it, news agencies had an equivalent status to editorial boards, publishers, or distributors. The first decree concerning the status of ITAR was published only in 1992. It defined ITAR as the central information agency of the Russian Federation for domestic and international audiences (Ob informatsionnom telegrafnom agentstve Rossii [ITAR] 1993). The later special decrees of the Russian government gave state-owned news agencies certain advantages, but did not regulate private agencies. Because of the slow pace of legislation, except for the general law on private firms, the private agencies could take advantage of the lack of regulation on their operations.

Both ITAR-TASS and RIA-Novosti were placed under the direct control of the president of the Russian Federation on December 22, 1994 (Lutz and Jankowski 1998, 64). However, government officials themselves appeared unsure of what to do with Novosti (APN), which used to provide feature services and photographs to promote the Soviet image abroad. A new agency, *Rossiiskoe informatsionnoe agentstvo* (RIA), was created to serve the interests of the new Russian Federation and, specifically, the political interests of Yeltsin against those of Gorbachev. After the coup, Novosti (APN) was closed, and its more than one hundred foreign correspondence bureaus were eliminated. RIA continued as a hot-line agency providing daily domestic news coverage (Volin 1999).

The idea of merging TASS and Novosti (APN) to form a joint stock company was debated but, when private investment failed to appear, Novosti (APN) was changed first, in 1993, into RIA and, in 1994, into a stock company, RIA-Novosti, owned by the state. In the latest decree of May 1998, RIA-Novosti was renamed Russian Information Agency Vesti, operating under the All-Russian State-Run Television and Radio Broadcasting Company (VGTRK)—consisting of the state-owned television, Radio Russia, Radio Maiak and ninety local television stations—thus remaining under state ownership. The government appoints the board chairperson and his/her deputies (Lutz and Jankowski 1998, 64). RIA-Novosti has had five chairpersons since 1993, a fact that reveals the difficulties the agency has faced during these years.

The Problems of State-Owned News Agencies

The problem of finding new funds for both ITAR-TASS and RIA-Novosti has remained unsolved. ITAR-TASS now receives 60 percent of its funding from the state budget and 40 percent from sales revenues. As a result, the number of staff dropped from 5,000 to about 2,000 in 1999; 550 of the remaining staff were journalists. The number of foreign correspondents first dropped from 108 to 58 (Rantanen and Vartanova 1995, 214), but has since been increased again to 100 in 1999 (Ignatenko 1999). The increase suggests that ITAR-TASS is again attempting to become a global agency.

The old Novosti (APN) received $100 million annually as a state subsidy, but the new RIA-Novosti was allocated only $1.9 million from the budget in 1998. In 1999, $4.5 million was granted to RIA-Novosti for its foreign operations—about 70 percent of its foreign budget and about 30 percent of its domestic budget. It has also faced a staff cut—only 600 out of 1,100 employees will remain ("Staff cuts at RIA Novosti" 1998, 11; Volin 1999).

Most of RIA-Novosti's highly specialized departments have been combined to form the Main Information Directorate (GDI), which works in three main areas—foreign news, domestic news, and the provision of information to the VGTRK media holding company which was entrusted to RIA-Novosti (without funding) ("Staff cuts at RIA Novosti" 1998, 10–11). There are few opportunities for RIA to find new customers. It has tried to establish new forms of service provision such as business news, videos, magazines, and consulting management companies. Again, a new solution—to transform RIA-Novosti into a news and advertising agency—was considered in 1998 ("Staff cuts at RIA Novosti" 1998, 11), but in 1999, RIA-Novosti returned to the old Novosti (APN) concept by reestablishing its foreign correspondent network and still providing a basic domestic news service. It gives its services free of charge to the partners of the VGTRK; as a result, television news broadcasts use RIA-Novosti as a source much more often than the press (Volin 1999).

The new financial situation of news agencies in postcommunist countries is particularly vulnerable after years of subsidization. State subsidies have dropped substantially in postcommunist countries; in 1997 Hungary retained only 35 percent of the earlier state subsidies, and in the Czech Republic, only 7 to 8 percent were retained (Rantanen 1998, 132). All postcommunist countries face a situation in which they have to find new sources of revenue. The problem, of course, is that after the liberalization of the market, the state agencies no longer hold a monopoly, but face competition from new entrants, both foreign and domestic. Because of their role in nation building, foreign ownership of state agencies is considered inconceivable. Turning to advertising is not an option, because news agencies do not reach the audience directly, as other media do.

The problem of finding new sources of revenue is not limited to postcommunist agencies. Wherever national news agencies engage in new revenue-producing activities, they step on the toes of other media (their clients). The most successful agencies, such as Reuters, are the ones that receive most of their revenue from non-media sources, an option not easily available to postcommunist agencies because of Reuters' dominant market position in Central and Eastern Europe (Rantanen 1998, 135).

Traditionally, clients provide news agencies—whatever their form of ownership or location—with their major source of income. When there is only one national news agency that has a monopoly position, it can set the prices. Often, as was the case of state-owned agencies in communist countries, the price did not necessarily have to meet the actual costs, which were covered by state subsidies. Nevertheless, when state subsidies diminished substantially, the only other source of income left was that from clients. In this sense, state-owned news agencies became increasingly dependent on the media market, a change that had more immediate impact on the old state-owned agencies.

In Russia, five new factors make it difficult for ITAR-TASS to increase its revenues and become financially more independent from the state. First, like other media in the world, Russian media have encountered the phenomena of sensationalism and tabloidization ("Sredstva massovoi informatsii Rossii" 1997, 30–31). A quest for serious news, foreign or domestic, is not necessarily a priority for the new Russian media (Rantanen and Vartanova 1995, 217).

Second, since the biggest Russian media now have direct contact with foreign agencies and media, ITAR-TASS is no longer the sole provider of foreign news. For example, in 1978, a one-week news sampling showed that 53 percent of foreign news published in *Izvestiia* came from TASS, while no news was published from Western agencies (Rantanen 1980, 53). In contrast, in 1995, a two-day news sampling revealed that no foreign news (of eight items) published in *Izvestiia* came from ITAR-TASS (Törmänen 1997, 97).

Third, there has been increasing competition from new domestic entrants. The new private agencies could provide a product that, especially in the early years after their foundation, was considered better than that of ITAR-TASS's. Foreign and domestic clients first turn to private agencies. Although ITAR-TASS and RIA-Novosti are still the leading agencies in the domestic market, they have to share it with other agencies, including Interfax (Rantanen and Vartanova 1995, 215–16).

Fourth, the structure of the press itself has changed dramatically since the Soviet era. For example, the circulation of major newspapers has dropped by millions. In 1992, the joint circulation of the central Moscow editions numbered one hundred million copies, whereas it is now only seven million ("Sredstva massovoi informatsii Rossii" 1998, 8–19; Y. Zassoursky 1998, 24). What this means in practice is that, if clients pay according to their circulation (meaning small media pay less than big media), there are fewer higher-paying customers.

Fifth, regional and local presses are rapidly developing ("Sredstva massovoi informatsii Rossii" 1998, 9, 12–13; Y. Zassoursky 1998, 24). Thus, the number of clients is potentially increasing, but individual clients' sizes are relatively small and have different needs than the big media. This is a factor that also works for ITAR-TASS's benefit—it still has the largest domestic correspondent network. According to several studies, ITAR-TASS provided more news from Russia and the Commonwealth of Independent Nations than any other agency (Rantanen and Vartanova 1993, 14; Törmänen 1997, 110; Mochenov 1998, 6). However, small regional agencies compete with ITAR-TASS for the same market.

Table 4.1   Quotations from Different Agencies in the Russian Press in 1997

Agency	Quotations in the central and Muscovite press	Share (%)	Quotations in the regional press	Share (%)
ITAR-TASS	15,066	64.6	5,914	55.7
RIA-Novosti	1,753	7.5	2,426	22.8
Interfax	6,497	27.9	2,281	21.5
Total	23,316	100.0	10,621	100.0

Source: Mochenov 1998, 6.

These factors do not always work against ITAR-TASS. Surprisingly, together with RIA-Novosti, ITAR-TASS has been the most popular among Russian media, especially among newspapers (Rantanen and Vartanova 1995, 215–17; Volin 1999). There are several explanations for ITAR-TASS's and RIA-Novosti's popularity. First, despite the private agencies' new image, what most media need is a daily agenda of news, the basic raw data concerning the operations of different governmental institutions. Second, local media need regional news, and the size of the network of local and regional correspondents is germane. Traditionally, ITAR-TASS's domestic network has not faced the cuts its foreign network has. Third, ITAR-TASS still has a monopoly over foreign news. No other domestic agency transmits foreign news to Russia. In times of financial crises, domestic media tend to choose the most inexpensive source. ITAR-TASS is considered the basic agency, in both prosperous and lean times, and the one that is chosen by default if media cannot afford more than one source.

The Position of Private Agencies

At present, there are three different kinds of news agencies in Russia: (1) national; (2) regional; and (3) specialized agencies. The first category consists of the state-owned ITAR-TASS and RIA-Novosti, and the privately owned Interfax. They all deliver political and financial news to their clients, both in Russia and abroad. These are the "big three" in the Russian news market. The regional agencies primarily collect political news and distribute it to regional clients that are mainly media, but can also be local authorities, who in turn supply news to the agencies. The specialized agencies deliver mostly economic news, but also concentrate on certain topics, such as entertainment news (Rantanen and Vartanova 1997).

Mikhail Komissar (1992), one of the journalists who founded Interfax in 1989 while he was still working in *Gosteleradio*, the state-owned broadcasting company, described the origins of the agency:

I used my contacts there, for example with Mr. Yakovlev and Gorbachev. I told Mr. Yakovlev: "I want to organize a news agency here to transmit news about perestroika." First the idea was to collect news, to copy it and after that fifty couriers would take it to foreign embass-

ies. We were journalists, specially prepared to write for foreigners. It is
a different thing to write for foreigners than for Russians.

Gosteleradio did not have money, for it was a state organization
with a rigid budget. We needed some money to start. I visited several
foreign firms like Agfa and they all refused because there was TASS.
Then I met Leo Weinberg, a businessman who was general manager of
the firm Interquadro. It had a lot of money, computers from Taiwan
. . . I asked him for $30,000 and several hundred thousand rubles.
Using my contacts with the Kremlin, I finally organized a contract
between the department of information at Gosteleradio and Interquadro. It was not an [independent] company, it belonged to Gosteleradio. We did not think about the company, our main idea was to earn
some money for Gosteleradio.

There are several keys to Interfax's success in Komissar's statement. First, at the time the agency was established, founding an
enterprise with a relatively small capital was still possible. The origi-
nal company was founded as part of Gosteleradio, and was only later
established as an independent company. The whole idea that a news
agency could be a private, profit-making enterprise, of course, was
quite revolutionary. Second, Interfax introduced the Western concept
of news into the domestic news agency business in Russia. It did not
inherit the burdens of the past—the rigid organizational structure of
TASS, or the Soviet concept of news. That staff could effectively use
its experience with foreign audiences acquired by operating inside
Gosteleradio made Interfax's founders fully aware of the differences
between Soviet and Western news criteria. Third, Interfax further
secured its financial position by concentrating not only on media clients, but also on nonmedia clients, including embassies and firms.
Finally, Interfax established close relations with the leading politicians of the opposition parties, including Boris Yeltsin, who later
came to power. With these contacts, the agency could secure its
access to privileged information that was previously only available to
TASS and, then, reach even further, to the information that was not
accessible to any medium in the country.

The other pioneering private agency, Postfactum, was also established with foreign capital. Its founders were the Fakt cooperative
(the commercial news organization of one of the biggest and most
authoritative alternative newspapers of the time, Kommersant), the
Soros Fund, and private persons including G. Pavlovsky, a well-

known figure who in the 1970s published the dissident journal *Poiski*. The statutory fund of the agency was approximately U.S. $100,000 (Manaev 1993, 76). A couple of years ago Postfactum ended its operations because of financial difficulties (Avdeenko and Pikser 1999, 18).

There are several smaller private news agencies currently operating in Russia. Since 1990, the Department of Registration at the State Press Committee of the Russian Federation has registered nearly 170 news agencies as media enterprises. However, there is no reliable information on how many are still operating in the market. Most of the private news services specialize in their home regions. For example, *Severo-Zapad* provides news from the northwestern parts of Russia to the St. Petersburg media, while *Ural-aktsept* operates in the Ural region. These agencies have different functions and organizational structures. Some are information departments inside newspapers (such as *Nega* and *Nevskoie vremiia*); others are radio stations (*Ekho Moskvy* AM radio station) that also sell their news to outside subscribers (Rantanen and Vartanova 1997).

The number of newspapers concentrating on financial news and business has grown rapidly in Russia since the early 1990s. As a result, there is a niche for agencies that gather and distribute only financial news for media and non-media customers. The first agencies to concentrate on financial news were founded in 1990–1991, when the first private banks were established, and the privatization of the Russian economy began. Usually, 85 percent of the clients of these agencies consist of banks and financial enterprises, 10 percent of insurance and audit companies, and 5 percent of privatized enterprises (Rantanen and Vartanova 1997).

The development of the Prime agency, which specializes in the distribution of financial news, reflects a new tendency in the news agency market. Established as a private company in 1993, Prime signed an agreement with the Central Bank of Russia to distribute its financial information. In September 1996, it set up a joint company with ITAR-TASS business service to distribute financial news. The new service, under the name Prime-TASS, serves former clientele of private and state news agencies. Both agencies benefited from the merger. Prime uses the networks of ITAR-TASS's foreign correspondent bureau, while ITAR-TASS hopes to improve its management and market appearance by implementing the experience of the private news agency (Rantanen and Vartanova 1997).

Although Interfax has secured its place among the "big three" in Russia, alongside with ITAR-TASS and RIA-Novosti, there are factors working against it and other private agencies. There is no doubt, as previously described, that, despite its deficiencies, ITAR-TASS enjoys a unique position in the market. Also, any Russian national news agency needs close contacts with government circles. As Komissar's interview reveals, from the beginning these contacts were essential to the establishment of Interfax. But more importantly, they are needed to gain access to government information. In Russia, where there is no tradition of the right to information, one has to know the right people inside the right government circles to gain information. Finally, the shift from a small exclusive news service to an agency that provides a full service is not an easy one, especially in an expanded, competitive environment in which foreign agencies are important rivals. Komissar of Interfax has complained how Western media buy the best Russian journalists with salaries far above those in Russian media (Yrjämä-Rantinoja 1992). The small communication technology (such as E-mail or faxes) used by private agencies also sets limits to their growth (Rantanen and Vartanova 1995, 218).

Foreign Agencies Enter the Market

Foreign agencies first focused their attention on the Soviet Union in the era of *perestroika*, when the country became a hot world story. The agencies increased their staff to improve their coverage during this period. When the contractual obligation to disseminate their services through TASS ended in the early 1990s, foreign agencies expanded their operations in Russia (Rantanen and Vartanova 1995, 217). Reuters has been the most active nondomestic agency in Russia and in most CEE (Central and Eastern European) countries. For example, as early as in 1994, the Reuters staff in Moscow alone exceeded 110, of whom three-quarters were Russian. As Michael Palmer has observed, Reuters no longer needs a Russian agency partner (1998, 188). Many stations and networks, such ITN News, ABC News, BBC World, *Deutsche Welle*, and CNN, also started to transmit news broadcasts to Russian stations. Although many of them have ceased to do so, the imported Western news values and styles became familiar to the Russian audience (Lutz and Jankowski 1998, 69).

Reuters has also been the most active supplier of financial news. In 1995, it launched a Russian-language economic news service using Cyrillic characters, which also competes with domestic general news services from Russian agencies. Its presence in Russia, and in other CEE countries, prevents national agencies from successfully expanding their activities into financial news services (see Palmer et al. 1998; Rantanen 1998).

The biggest change that has taken place since the days of *perestroika*, however, is the gradual adoption of Western news styles by private and foreign agencies. TASS, seldom a style setter, was forced to follow the others' example. It was private and foreign agencies that set the standard of news writing in contemporary Russia.

THE FUTURE OF STATE-OWNED NEWS AGENCIES

State-owned news agencies have traditionally been seen as one of the bulwarks protecting "national interests" against the incursion of foreign news agencies. This has been especially true in Russia, where, even in the nineteenth century, the state intervened when the German agency, Wolff, became too powerful in the Russian market (Rantanen 1990). Times are now different, but the question of the protection of national interests is sometimes still discussed in the language of the nineteenth century. As the director of the first state-owned agency wrote in 1904, the agency was "to develop its own program independently and in a fashion that corresponds to the interests of Russia" (Rantanen 1990, 131). In 1917, the new Soviet agency ROSTA (later TASS) was strictly supervised by the People's Commissariat of Foreign Affairs (Rantanen 1994, 10). Almost eighty years later, the newspaper *Obschaia Gazeta* published an article entitled "The Slaves of Reuters," written by one of the executives of ITAR-TASS, and thus reflecting the official policy of the agency. The author of the article bitterly complained about Reuters' increasing influence in the Russian news market and ITAR-TASS's inability to compete with it (Poroikov 1995). He wrote:

Not by accident, in many countries measures have been taken to forbid, in general, Reuters' independent operations in their territories.

Reuters—a powerful financial corporation—that does not only dominate the sphere of information, but, above all, limits all economic possibilities.

In this way, AFP, DPA [Deutsche Presse Agentur] are currently developing in Russia. The AFP has established in Moscow a large bureau in which 150 people work. Now they are interested in our Far East. In Russia, in the CIS, Moscow is a bridgehead to conquer our market. Our information space is absolutely open; Russian hopes and interests are not taken into consideration; all these agencies can operate here as they like. This is the whole story. In this way alien, information empires are created in our territory.

In his first interview after his appointment as the new general director of ITAR-TASS in 1995, Vitaly Ignatenko said that he was more worried about the activities of the Western agencies that "freely operate in the Russian news market than about the situation of the Russian media." He also expressed his willingness to limit the activities of Western agencies in Russia (Pishikova 1995). Two years later, Ignatenko again repeated that protecting ITAR-TASS from foreign competitors remained among his first priorities (Loshchak 1997).

Not surprisingly, the state is still seen as the most powerful protector of national news agencies. It is difficult to imagine that media struggling with financial difficulties would assume the task. In 1998, the representatives of the Communist Party of the Russian Federation faction in the Duma sent a letter to the Prime Minister proposing that an "organizational propaganda center for the state mass media be set up on the basis of the RIA-Novosti news agency." The letter suggested that the project could be financed from the state budget, with additional private capital and funding from the agency itself. The Duma majority also proposed the establishment of a separate RIA-Novosti Board of Trustees consisting of representatives of the government, both chambers of Parliament, and even the Supreme Court. Moreover, the board would draw on Duma and ministerial experience and on the Foreign Intelligence Service and the Federal Security Service ("Communists call for state 'media propaganda center' " 1998, 10).

The Communist Party's arguments raise the question of creating and protecting national image and interests in both domestic and foreign news transmission. Their argument about domestic news is "the constant propaganda influence of the private mass media in the regions, which certainly do not promote national and federal interests," while in foreign news there is "the task to create a favourable image in order to achieve Russia's foreign policy and foreign economic goals" ("Communists call for state 'media propaganda center' " 1998, 10).

Although the Communist Party represents an extreme position in its desire to combine news transmission and propaganda, it is easy to see from where these arguments come. The tradition of the state-owned or -supported national news agency has a long history. The new era of globalization raises, as it did in the nineteenth century, the question of how the domestic market can be protected. However, the history of previous Russian state-owned agencies should ring warning bells when the attempts are made to find the solution in the past.

CONCLUSION

News agencies have combined a dual global and national role since their beginnings in the nineteenth century; the exception is Reuters, which always operated primarily as a global agency. Others, such as the agencies in Imperial Russia whose activities were regulated by strict censorship, had to adjust to the situation in which the French Havas, the German Wolff, and the British Reuters formed an international alliance of news exchange. Despite their size, news agencies in Imperial Russia and in the Soviet Union never were able to compete with major Western agencies. Censorship and state/party interests always stood in the way if Russian news agencies tried to follow the criteria set by Western agencies. For example, the requirement of speed is not compatible with the internal demand to control every in- and outgoing news item.

If news agencies in Imperial Russia had difficulties in adjusting to the requirements of the international exchange that demanded fast and reliable news, TASS and Novosti (APN) (less so because of its concentration on soft news and features) in the Soviet Union found it even more problematic. After the Second World War, when the Soviet Union achieved a superpower status, its news agency had to meet international standards and become an international agency itself. It was a source of national pride and prestige that TASS was a member of the "Big Five," a member of the consortium whose other members were leading Western agencies. Of course, TASS was different, because it did not operate in the same way as its Western counterparts, but its status was high. When TASS made announcements, it was the Soviet government speaking through its official representative to other nations of the world. TASS became an important voice not only for the Soviet Union, but also for the whole communist part of the world.

Nevertheless, this status paralyzed TASS. It could not develop as a news organization, because the demands of modern news transmission (such as speed and accuracy) did not meet the demands of a government agency, which often had the function of preventing news delivery about, for example, nuclear disasters or dissident activities. TASS was too close to the government and the party to be able to change. It was a huge organization, and the appointments were often made, especially at the top, on purely political grounds. It is no wonder that TASS was not among the media organizations that started to change before the system collapsed. The change had to come from outside, as it did when the first private news agencies were founded, and when global agencies such as Reuters started their own direct news service.

But what was to be done with TASS and Novosti (APN) when the system collapsed? In many postcommunist countries, news agencies changed but, for the most part, remained in state ownership. National media with their diverse, clashing, and possibly foreign interests rarely assumed the responsibility of maintaining a national service in any Central and Eastern European country (Rantanen 1998, 135). The situation in Russia differs from other postcommunist countries in that it is the only country that has two state-owned agencies competing against each other. There are several explanations for this.

First, there is, of course, the sheer size of the market. Russia is a potentially rich market, despite its financial difficulties, that provides news service for over 147 million people. In principle, it is possible to find a niche for every agency. Second, because of the political power struggle inside the Russian state, each group needs its own agency. History has shown that in times of political crisis the existence of only one agency is too risky. In 1917, Bolshevik forces seized all strategic points in St. Petersburg, including railway stations, bridges, the telephone company, the national bank, the telegraph, and the Petro-grad Telegraph Agency (Rantanen 1994, 8). The same situation would not be possible in the twenty-first century because there are too many agencies and media to be captured. The maintenance of the state-owned agencies guarantees that no political group controls every agency, including Interfax. This raises the third point—the definition of a state agency.

The difference between state-owned and private agencies is not clear-cut in Russia. Interfax could not have survived without its con-nections with the government circles. There are different kinds of state agencies, such as the French AFP or the Spanish EFE, whose integrity and independence are not called into question because they are state supported. A Russian AFP or EFE could be a perfectly plau-sible option. As Boyd-Barrett and Rantanen have pointed out, in principle, although sometimes with difficulties, a national agency can make a good job of being both a government information service and a media service (2000, 97). To achieve this goal, agencies and govern-ments should reach a consensus as to what tasks outside the range of normal provision could most usefully be undertaken by agencies, without further sacrificing their credibility. What counts at the end of the day is to have a news service that is comprehensive, fast, and accurate, as well as being a source of information as to the govern-ment's position on important issues.

Unfortunately, present state-owned agencies in post-Communist Russia have been too close to state power to reinvent themselves radi-cally in the global era. Further, unlike Reuters, they must again try to promote the national image both at home and abroad. Both ITAR-TASS and RIA-Novosti have again been given more state support to create and expand their foreign correspondent network (Ignatenko 1999; Volin 1999). This also indicates that Russian news agencies, despite their present orientation to the national, are also trying to win back their previous position as a member of the "Big Five." To win back the position would help to repair Russia's present status as a fallen superpower. It would also mean that post-Communist Russia would be less dependent on Western sources in covering the events in its own territory.

An examination of Russian state-owned news agencies reveals the persistence and continuity of old traditions in the face of fundamen-tal political and economical change. It has been very difficult to reform "the old." The closer the old is to national interests, the more difficult it is to reform it. Although the agencies have adopted some Western styles of news presentation, they have remained primarily national. Their task is to promote Russian interests, as it was previously to promote Soviet interests. In the highly competitive environment in which other news agency major players have disentangled themselves from the promotion of their national interests, Russian state-owned agencies have shown little sign of moving from the national to the global. Today, as previously, they serve more national interests than global interests. This, in turn, again gives evidence for the strength of the national, even in the times of "high" globalization. The Russian state-owned news agencies are good examples of how globalization is overcome by national interests.

5

Television

Chris Barker writes that there is little doubt that television is a global phenomenon: there are 750 million television sets in more than 160 countries watched by 2.5 billion people every day (1997, 27). Not surprisingly, much of the debate on the effects of cultural globalization has concentrated on the role of television. However, research on television has demonstrated not only its role in the process of globalization, but also how television continues to remain regional, national, and local at the same time. As Sinclair et al. argue, "global, regional, national, and even local circuits of program exchange overlap and interact in a multi-faceted way, no doubt with a great variety of cultural effects, which are impossible to conceptualize within the more concentric perspective appropriate to previous decades" (1996, 5).

Although there has been agreement among communication scholars about the importance of doing research on the role of television in different parts of the world, virtually no attention has been given to its globalization in Russia, the world's third largest television market (Hoskins et al. 1997, 38). This has much to do with researchers' reluctance to do research on non-Western countries. To quote Curran and Park, "theorists survey the universe while never straying from the international airport" (2000, 11). While theorists were thus occupied, a major change took place in the Russian television market after the Soviet Union collapsed—Russian television became globalized.

There is very little information or analysis available on the global elements in Soviet television; however, the data that is available confirms the magnitude of the change from almost entirely national to global television programming. The classic study for UNESCO by Nordenstreng and Varis in 1974 demonstrated the dominance of U.S. television program exports around the world. What was also revealed by the study, but received much less attention, was that the former Soviet Union was a self-reliant television producer that imported fewer programs than, for example, Great Britain. It was also the main exporter of television programs to Eastern Europe. In 1974 in the former Soviet Union, only 5 percent of the programs were of foreign origin. At the same time, such countries as Bulgaria and the GDR imported two-thirds of their programs from the Soviet Union (Nordenstreng and Varis 1974, 12, 25). Ten years later, the Soviet Union still imported only 8 percent of its programs, while twenty-one percent of the imported programs in Eastern Europe came from the Soviet Union (Varis 1984, 148).

In 1997, of all Russian television programs, 60 percent were imported, and all serials were of foreign origin. The exchange of programs among Central and Eastern European television stations has almost ceased. For example, American programs comprise about half of the foreign content on Polish television, while the share of Russian programs is 0.4 percent (Jakubowicz 1998, 259–60). The change from an exporter to an importer puts post-Communist Russia in the same category as many other countries that import most of their television programs and export very little.

We are not only talking about the globalization of television, but also about the globalization of electronic culture in post-Communist Russia. At the same time, with the high tide of the globalization of television in the late 1980s and early 1990s, Russian domestic film production also dramatically fell. In 1990, 215 Soviet and 178 foreign films were released in the Soviet Union. In 1995, 82 Russian films were released, and another 35 from the former Soviet Republics. The number of films from other countries, of which the overwhelming majority were from the United States, was 169 (Graffy 1998, 191). As Julian Graffy points out, the video industry, meanwhile, was thriving, with video salons being set up to show pirated copies of films that had sometimes not been released to cinemas (1998, 189). Between 1986 and 1991, total cinema attendance fell from 4 billion to 2.5 billion, and there were an estimated 14 million unsold seats a day. Tickets sales in movie theaters in 1996 declined to one-fifteenth of the 1990 total, and the theaters that remained open filled, on average, only 3 to 8 percent of their seats. The available data indicates that, in 1995, Russia ranked lowest among European countries in its sale of movie tickets per capita, averaging less than one ticket per citizen (Larsen 1999, 193).

The fall in the production of cinema production and attendance coincided with the birth of a new video culture that had begun in the 1980s. As shown in chapter 3, videos were mainly exported from the West and provided a counterculture to Soviet television. After the collapse of Communism, the video market continued to grow, although it did not serve the same function as before, since television had started also to show Western films. In the first half of the 1990s, post-Soviet Russia experienced a high tide of globalization, which in electronic culture was mainly Westernization, even Americanization.

This major cultural shift has failed to attract the attention of globalization theorists, whatever their approach or school is. In principle, we can divide cultural globalization into two theories—homogenization and heterogenization. Both schools have neglected Russia for different reasons. First, the notion of cultural or media imperialism is considered a profoundly Western phenomenon into which Soviet hegemony in Eastern Europe never quite fit. This happened despite the fact that Boyd-Barrett, in his famous media imperialism article, wrote that "we need to know a great deal more about media systems relations in the Communist bloc, whether and to what

Table 5.1   Top 10 Videotapes in Moscow in 1997

1	Саботаж	Sabotage
2	Крикуны	Screamers
3	Брат	Brat (Russia)
4	Ермак	Yermak (Russia)
5	Майкп	Michael
6	Драйв	Drive
7	Джерри Магуайр	Jerry Maguire
8	Люди в черном	Men in Black
9	Взрыв	Blust
10	Фанат	Fanat

Source: Moscow VIDEO Market Report 1997, www.geocities.com/Hollywood/Theater/2902/

extent these are similar relations in the Western sphere of influence, and also whether Western media influence can be said to have penetrated Communist systems and with what consequences" (1977, 134). Second, globalization heterogenization theories have mainly focused on emerging new regional centers (Asia), but have paid little attention to the ones in decline. Hence, no matter what position one takes, the countries that do not fit into the theories, such as post-Communist Russia, are excluded from globalization debates.

As a result, we need to ask whether the available theories and concepts can be used at all in our consideration of Russia. It is not a center, it is not a periphery; it is developed, but it is not continuing to do so. We need to return to the theories and concepts used in earlier studies and see whether there are any elements that can be used in trying to analyze the cultural transformation taking place in post-Communist Russia.

THREE WAVES OF INTERNATIONAL COMMUNICATION THEORIES

Annabelle Sreberny-Mohammadi divides international communication into three different paradigms that have dominated the field: (1) communications and development; (2) cultural imperialism; and (3) cultural pluralism (1996, 178). Each of the paradigms concentrates on different aspects of media and communications. The communications and development paradigm is mainly concerned about technology, while cultural imperialism is mainly about the structures and content. The cultural pluralism paradigm represents a shift to audience and reception. According to Sreberny-Mohammadi, communications and development theorists, who dominated in the 1960s, suggested that the traditional values of the developing world were the central obstacles to political participation and economic activity, the two key elements of the development process (1996, 178–79). The solutions were to increase communications ("the more communication, the better"), and to promote the use of communications media to alter attitudes and values.

As Sreberny-Mohammadi observes (1996, 179), this perspective has been roundly criticized for its ethnocentrism, its ahistoricity, its linearity, for conceiving of development in an evolutionary, endogenist fashion, and for solutions that actually enforced dependency rather than helping to overcome it. In the case of the Soviet Union, communications and development theories became close to propaganda theories that considered the role of communications vital to the spread of communist ideology. The Communist Party always saw media and communications as tools of propaganda. The more media and communications, the better, as long as it was in the hands of the party and government; nondomestic communications and media were considered dangerous.

The second intellectual paradigm was cultural imperialism, whose theorists saw globalization as a one-way process—Westernization/ Americanization or imperialism that threatened to overwhelm national cultures. Cees Hamelink talks about synchronization— when the traffic of cultural products goes massively in one direction, and has basically a synchronic mode in which the whole process of local social inventiveness and cultural creativity may be thrown into confusion or is definitely destroyed (1983, 56). Boyd-Barrett defined media imperialism as "the process whereby the ownership, structure, distribution, or content of the media in any one country are singly or together subject to substantial external pressures from media interests of any other country or countries without proportionate reciprocation of influence by the country so affected" (1977, 117–18). For Boyd-Barrett, the two elements of invasion and imbalance in power resources justify the use of the term imperialism.

Boyd-Barrett writes that the country which is affected by media influence either adopts this influence as a deliberate commercial or political strategy, or simply absorbs this influence unreflectively as the result of the contract (1997, 119). According to him, the overall context of power imbalance, within which media activities occur and are transmitted, indicates that far greater freedom of choice or option accompanies the process of export and dissemination than the process of adoption and absorption. Boyd-Barrett admits that, because the term "media imperialism" refers to the transmission of media influence, both to relatively developed as well as to the so-called Third World countries, and because there are differences in gross wealth even between countries of the latter category, it would be a mistake to exclude the factor of political discretion at the receiving end of media influence.

Ullamaija Kivikuru has elaborated Boyd-Barrett's analysis. The main modes of foreign dependency (which can also been seen in Western European, developed countries such as Finland) for media are import (media content, processing structures, technical equipment) and adoption, or absorption, which consist of "modes of operation or administration from abroad" (Kivikuru 1998, 12). Kivikuru mentions the emergence of "mini-BBC's" in former British colonies as a fairly typical example of adoption. She defines absorption as "gliding" into new structures and practices without deliberate decision-making. Kivikuru asserts that modeling is the main form of mass-media dependency, even in industrialized countries (1988, 13).

As Sreberny-Mohammadi observes, like the earlier arguments for communications and development, the cultural imperialism model was based on a situation of comparative media scarcity, limited global players, and embryonic media systems in much of the Third World (1996, 180). Again, the Soviet Union did not fit the theory—it was not a developing country that was defenseless against imperialist powers; the Soviet Union was a superpower that had done exactly what development theorists had suggested—it had created a strong national media and communications system that "protected" its citizens against Western media imperialism, and practiced its own form of media imperialism in Central and Eastern Europe.

In contrast to homogenization theorists, the cultural pluralists saw globalization as heterogenization, the mixture of the global and the local. They also saw local cultures as capable of resisting or opposing Westernization. Since the cultural pluralists are much more interested in audiences than institutions, the multiple forms of reception are considered a key element in the glocalization process. This is not only due to the capability of local cultures to resist, but also to the fact that globalization is not solely understood as Westernization. First, there are more global players than there were before. In television, the import of Brazilian and Mexican telenovelas and Indian films into different parts of the world are the most common examples of counter-, or reversed, flows. Second, the importance of the national has declined, and increasingly, researchers refer to the local instead of the national. The role of the local is seen much more powerful than that of the national. Cultural globalization theorists refer to glocalization, melangenization, or hybridization of the global and the local. Third, Appadurai (1996, 32) makes a distinction between globalization and homogenization with his concept of indigenization. He writes that "at least as rapidly as forces from various metropolises are brought into new societies they tend to become indigenized in one or another way" (1996, 32). In this process the media play a crucial role.

Appadurai further distinguishes between "hard" and "soft" cultural forms (1996, 90). Hard cultural forms are those that come with links between value, meaning, and embodied practice, forms that are difficult to break and hard to transform. Soft cultural forms, by contrast, are those that permit relatively easy separation of embodied performance from meaning and value, and relatively successful transformation at each level. Television could easily be seen as a soft cultural form and a medium that traditionally (outside the Communist bloc) has been global. Fourth, relating to the third point, indigenization takes place partly by consumption, a factor that was completely neglected by earlier theorists. Meanings cannot be imported, as such, but are negotiated by audiences in their own localities. Interestingly, Featherstone distinguishes absorption/assimilation strategies in relation to globalization using the same terms as Boyd-Barrett and Kivikuru, but adding resistance to his strategies (1995, 116).

When we think of the three approaches to globalization, it is easy to point out their inadequacies in relation to post-Communist Russia. Never before have we had a historical situation in which a former communist cultural superpower falls on its knees and is forced to open its strictly protected sphere to global cultural products. In contrast to developing countries, the Soviet Union had a relatively developed media system, especially its television, which reached 97 percent of the households. However, despite this extensive reach and also because of it, global programs spread like soup due to television's nature as soft cultural form after the collapse of Communism—every channel started to show foreign programs simultaneously and they reached a mass audience. There was no time for a slow adjustment; the doors were opened to foreign programming almost instantaneously. In this sense, the change is even more dramatic than in other countries where globalization has, to use Kivikuru's term, glided in during several decades.

The homogenization theorists saw national media as being unable to defend themselves against foreign media. The cultural pluralists, on the other hand, saw the national as less important—the state withering away and resulting in a new binary position between the global and local. Interestingly, the latest generation of global media theorists has started to re-underline the importance of the national in contrast to both media imperialists and cultural pluralists. As James Curran and Myung-Jin Park observe, despite the internationalization of film, music, and news wholesaling, and despite the rise of transnational communications corporations and the growth of media export markets, communications systems are still, in significant respects, national (2000, 11–12). They list three reasons. First, different nations have different languages, political systems, power structures, cultural traditions, economies, international links, and histories. Second, the popular notion that most people watch American television programs is also unsupported by the evidence. Third, national states are influential in shaping media systems by licensing authorities and regulations of national television channels over which they have control.

Judging from the number of books and articles on global television, there seems to be an agreement that television is the most important medium. However, when we talk about the globalization of television, it is not only content that matters. As Barker has pointed out, it is not just a numerical issue, but is also concerned with the changing character of television—in particular, the growing organization of television along commercial, rather than public-service, lines (1997, 4). In a situation where the whole media system changes, as happened in postcommunist countries, it makes sense not only to look at contents, but at structures and audiences as well. In this way, we can combine the methods of analysis of different approaches, and see what works in analyzing postcommunist television.

THE STRUCTURAL CHANGES
IN RUSSIAN TELEVISION

When we analyze the globalization of the structure of Russian television, there are several factors we need to take into account. First, Russian television is both technologically and socially old. We are not talking about a developing country that has only started to build its national television network. In contrast to common belief, television in the Soviet Union started not much later than that in the United States. Regular television broadcasts started in Moscow as early as in 1931. In 1937, new centers were built in Moscow and

Leningrad, but the war postponed further development. In 1940, there were only 400 television sets in the Soviet Union; in 1950, there were 15,000; afterwards, television became widely socially accepted. In 1960, the number of television sets reached 4.8 million. Then, in the five years between 1965 and 1970, the availability of television sets was more than doubled. Television production jumped in the 1970s, and by 1976, Soviet industry was producing 7 million sets annually. In 1970, there were 34.8 million television sets; and in 1979, 70 million. By that time, there were 98 television sets per one hundred families (*Soviet Mass Media* 1979, 66). In 1960, only 5 percent of the Soviet population could watch television, but by 1986, 93 percent of the population were viewers, living in areas comprising more than 86 percent of the territory of the USSR (Mickiewitcz 1988, 3; Paasilinna 1995, 81).

Second, television was a highly controlled medium that was developed according to the interests of the state and the Communist Party. It was also a highly centralized medium. In the Soviet Union there were two national networks, First Program and Second Program, both controlled by the state and the Communist Party. The First Program carried the most important news—the events of the "highest significance"—while the Second Program played repeats from the First. For Moscow residents, there were three other network choices—Third and Fourth Programs, together with the Leningrad channel that was also available to Muscovites (Mickiewicz 1988, 7–8). However, even the Third and Fourth Programs did not offer any real alternatives, since they, too, were controlled by local authorities.

As noted in chapter 2, the first changes in the contents of television programs took place during the years of *perestroika*. The structural changes have taken a much longer time and have followed adoption or absorption from abroad, or modeling, as Kivikuru suggests. The pattern of ownership has changed substantially. In 1990–1991 all the television channels in Russia belonged to the state and were controlled by the State Committee for Broadcasting. In the following years the number of state-owned and state-controlled television companies have remained the same, but privately owned television stations now outnumber the state-owned companies by more than ten times. In the year 2000, the number of television stations numbered about 1,000 (Zassoursky and Vartanova 2000). Thus, in some cases, present Russian television has followed Western examples of ownership.

The rise of private ownership was not the only consequence of globalization. One of the consequences of the introduction of capitalism has been the concentration of media ownership. In Russia, there are now four media empires that own both print and electronic media, which sometimes work hand in hand with the government in broadcasting ("Sredstva massovoi informatsii Rossii" 1998; Vartanova 1997). There are six national channels. The old and the new are combined in different ways, not necessarily following forms of ownership. The reorganization of Russian central television began in 1990, when the state-owned Russian TV RTR was founded. It started broadcasting in April 1991 and became the Second Channel. On November 30, 1994, President Yeltsin signed a decree on "privatizing" the Ostankino Broadcasting Company, with the government owning 51 percent of the shares. The rest were in the hands of private shareholders, the largest being Boris Berezovsky, another of the new Russian media barons. The new entity, called Russian Public Television, ORT, took control and was responsible for programs on the First Channel from January 1, 1995 ("Yeltsin Approves Ostankino 'Privatization'" 1994). Berezovsky owned the shares until 2000, when after being threatened by authorities, he announced he would give them up. If Berezovsky did indeed give up the shares, ORT has again become state-controlled. In 1999, the government established a new national channel, Kultura, which produces and broadcasts cultural programs. Thus, there are three channels that are almost wholly state-owned.

Although the first private television channel appeared as early as 1990, the first private national channel, NTV, began its operations in 1993 and became the Fourth Channel. It is entirely privately owned by the Most Financial Group, controlled by Vladimir Gusinsky. It is Gusinsky's empire that has been providing alternative news about the war in Chechnya and corruption in the Kremlin. As a result, Gusinsky was arrested in the summer of 2000, for "financial reasons," but was later released. Two other new channels are available nationally: the Sixth Channel, TV-6, originally a joint venture between Russian interests and Ted Turner's TBS of Atlanta, now partly owned by Berezovsky; and TV-Centre, which started broadcasting in forty regions of the country in 1997. The Moscow City authorities own a 67 percent stake in TV-Centre (Mickiewicz 1997, 222).

Hence, Russian television has only partly adopted its forms of ownership from abroad. Current Russian television is a mixture of state- and privately owned stations. The result has not been exclusively private or state television, but joint ownerships of the state, cities (such as the Moscow City Council), and private capital. As Y. Zassoursky and Vartanova have noted, what is lacking is public television (2000)—the "mini BBC" was not imported to Russia.

The transformation has taken place in a "lawless" situation; so far there has been no broadcasting legislation, but the legal basis for broadcasting of radio and television programs is included in the Mass Media Act of 1992. The law has made setting up private media easier by granting a tax holiday to founders for the first two years. Individual citizens, associations, organizations, companies, and state organs can function as founders. As Michel P. Lutz and Jaromir Jankowski observe, "Fundamental aspects of broadcasting, such as the licensing of news or existing stations, or the scope and content of broadcast advertising, were not covered in the law, nor were the legal supervision of registered broadcasters or rights of ownership, including the extent of foreign capital holdings in Russian radio or television stations" (1998, 63). But, as Y. Zassoursky (2000) has remarked, the state has strengthened its control over television.

All six channels are national, but ORT and RTR have the most comprehensive reach, while the others vary considerably. Practically every Russian can watch ORT and RTR, about three-fourths have access to NTV, and 50 percent can watch TV-6. In big cities, viewers can have six channels, in addition to satellite and local channels. Still, 5.36 million people living in 18,684 cities, towns, and villages can receive only one television program ("Lazutkin Assesses the State of Russian TV" 1996, 12).

The funding of television has changed profoundly in post-Communist Russia, and again the result shows distinctive national features. While license fees have been the most common form of funding public broadcasting in Western Europe, they were unknown in the Soviet Union; today Russia lacks the infrastructure that is necessary to collect fees effectively. This left two other main forms of funding commonly used elsewhere in the world, parliamentary appropriation and advertising (Hoskins et al. 1997, 92–95), as options for Russia.

Figure 5.1   Sources of Information for the Russian Public

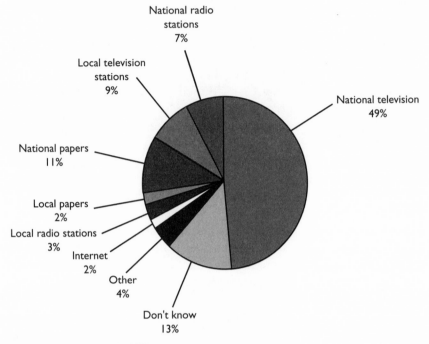

Source: *Izvestiia Media* March 26, 2001.

Although the Soviet state fully financed broadcasting, the Russian state is no longer interested in performing the task. For example, in 1996, RTR received only 30 percent of the promised budget money from the government (Kolesnik 1997, 11), while ORT has received no funding at all from the state since the government sold off 49 percent of its shares ("Paper Views Effects on ORT of Advertising crisis" 1998, 6). Thus, advertising was left as the major form of funding for broadcasting companies, despite the combined state-private ownership. The 1998 financial crises in Russia made their economic position even more vulnerable—when advertising revenue dropped dramatically, all television channels faced serious cuts in their budgets.

THE ENTERTAINIZATION OF CONTENTS

These structural changes have brought global elements into Russian television content. The emergence of new channels has multiplied the program time that must be filled. Domestic production could not instantaneously respond to the increasing demand for new types of programs, and the only alternative was to turn to foreign producers. Also, in the new competitive environment, there was no longer only one national broadcasting company buying foreign programs, with a de facto monopoly in the domestic market. Several companies were now competing for the same products that had to be purchased with advertising revenues.

When Communism started to collapse, Soviet, and later, Russian television were obliged to confront a global phenomenon called the "entertainization" of television, as did the countries of Central and Eastern Europe. It profoundly changed the ratio between different program categories. If one compares these categories in two different decades, this development is clear (see table 5.2).

Although the program categories of the two decades do not coincide exactly, entertainment, features, and television series occupied nearly half of the programs in 1997. Another study confirms the trend. In 1988, the First Channel of state television only devoted 8.8 percent of its transmission time to feature programs, but by 1993, its successor, Ostankino (ORT), broadcast features 20 percent of the time. A comparison of the program breakdown on the two RTR channels during 1994 and 1995 (with total transmission increasing by 30 percent) reveals important changes—the broadcasting time for fiction grew by 44 percent (with cartoons up by 176 percent); for entertainment, 192 percent; for light music, 128 percent; and for newscasts by 83 percent. On the other hand, transmission times for information programs and serious music fell by 61 percent and 28

Table 5.2   Program Categories in Russian Television

1986 (First Program)		1997 (ORT)	
Films	29%	Feature and Television Series	30%
Information/News	20%	News	20%
Culture	15%	Entertainment	16%
Production/Economy	12%	Children and Youth	14%
Government/History	9%	Sports	6%
Children's Programs	8%	Education	4%
Sports	4%	Other	5%
Science & Travel	3%		

Source: Mickiewicz 1988, 154; ORT.

percent, respectively. Education programs, which had a share of 14.3 percent, or 902 hours, only took up 23 hours in 1994 (Lutz and Jankowski 1998, 69).

The same phenomenon is even more apparent by looking at television schedules. Every channel follows the same scheduling order in its programming. The examples in table 5.3 are from May 24–31, 2000. The four channels, ORT, RTR, TVC, and NTV filled their primetime with entertainment (game shows) and serials and films, which have become an essential feature of Russian television. In this sense, Russian television has followed the patterns of Western television, and imported the new structures of television programming.

THE ORIGINS OF RUSSIAN
TELEVISION PROGRAMS

An increase in the number of imported programs accompanied the phenomenon of entertainization of Russian television. Some researchers have warned that indigenous audiovisual production is threatened with extinction in Central and Eastern Europe, given the amount of largely North American programs purchased to fill the schedules (Trappel and Mahon 1998, 15). This, too, is the case with

**Table 5.3   Serials and Films on Russian Prime-time Television
(7–9 P.M. and 10–11:30 P.M.)
TV Schedule for May 24–31, 2000**

TV Channel	Monday	Tuesday	Wednesday	Thursday	Friday	Saturday	Sunday
ORT	Serial; Serial	Talk Show; Film	Serial; Film	TV Show; Film	TV Game; Serial	Film; Concert	Film; Film
RTR	Serial; Film	Serial; TV Show	Serial; TV Show	Serial; TV Show	Serial; Film	TV Show; Film	Weekly News; Film
TVC	Film; Talk Show	Sport Show; Film	Serial; Talk Show	Film; Talk Show	Film; Talk Show	TV Game; Film	Concert; Film
NTV	Film; TV Show	Serial; Talk Show	Film; Football Match	Serial; Serial	Serial; TV Show	TV Show; Film	Weekly News; Film

post-Communist Russia's importation of soap operas for television. By September 2000, almost all soap operas were of foreign origin on Russian television. Their supply is similar to Western European countries, with the exception of the relatively high number of South American soap operas from Mexico, Argentina, Brazil, and Columbia. The latter are shown not only shown on ORT and RTR, but on local pay and cable TV channels as well (though not on NTV, which shows the American soap opera *Sunset Beach,* instead). Their low cost makes them ideal to fill program time if domestic low-cost production is not available.

In contrast to soap operas that are almost totally imported, there are domestic television serials, such as those shown by ORT and NTV, but most serials are from the United States and Great Britain. Serials in 1999 included *MacGyver, Murder She Wrote,* and *Inspector Derrick.*

As table 5.4 shows, although Western films dominate, old Soviet and new Russian films still comprised approximately half of all the films shown on Russian television in 1998. More foreign films were shown, but domestic films had not lost their share of television time. Old Soviet films were, in general, cheaper than foreign films, and it was possible to buy the rights for a whole package at a very low price.

In addition to the new composition of television programming and the import of foreign soap operas, serials, and films, globalization also operated on Russian television through the import of Western

Table 5.4   Origins of Films Shown on Russian TV on March 9–15, 1998

ORT	RTR	NTV	TVC
16 films	*6 films*	*15 films*	*17 films*
5 USSR	3 USSR	5 USSR	9 USSR
8 USA	1 Russia	1 USSR-Italy	1 USSR-Norway
1 Germany	1 Russia-France	5 USA	1 USSR-SFRIU
2 France	1 Italy-France	1 Spain	1 Russia-China
		1 UK-USA	1 Australia
		1 Ukraine	2 Russia
		1 France	1 USA
			1 India

Source: Vestnik televisionnoi informatsii 1998

formats. Many of the most popular programs, such as *Pole chudec* (*Wheel of Fortune*), *Ugadai melodiiu (Name That Tune)*, and *Chas Pik (Rush Hour,* a copy of *Larry King)* have imitated the formats of popular Western shows. This, of course, would be a perfect example of the modeling Kivikuru refers to (1988, 13), when a foreign format is adapted. However, these formats may also be evidence of indigenization of global products. The fact that game shows are being adjusted to national circumstances, by using national people and a national language, also shows how national media systems, or, as in this case, Russian television, perform their roles as filters between the global and the local.

There is another distinguishing feature that stands out in nationalizing the global. All foreign programs are dubbed. Russian viewers very seldom hear English spoken, since the voices of Russian actors are dubbed over the English-speaking actors. Russian television has willingly paid the high costs of dubbing—three times more expensive than subtitling (Lengyel 1998, 162)—which, however, are lower in Russia than in other countries because of the large size of the audience in Russia. This is one of the long-standing traditions on Soviet/ Russian television that has lived through societal changes. It may be something that has to do with the size of the country and the number of speakers. As Richard Collins has pointed out, large European countries (France, Italy, Germany, Spain) broadly prefer dubbing, whereas small countries (Belgium, Denmark, Finland, Greece, Netherlands, Norway, Portugal, and Sweden) prefer subtitling (1998, 176).

THE CONSUMPTION OF TELEVISION PROGRAMS

An accurate portrait of consumption of television programs has not been previously possible because of missing viewing data. But the advent of advertising and the de-monopolization of the market have resulted in several competing audience research organizations that now provide this data. Hence, it is now possible to compare the supply and consumption of television.

One of the most striking features is that the old channels have maintained their market position. It is not only a question of availability, but popularity, as well. ORT enjoys a popularity that exceeds

Table 5.5 Top Films on Russian Television in 1999

Film	Rating	Share
The Peculiarities of National Fishing (Russia)	23.8	57.0
Pretty Woman (USA)	20.7	50.1
Ivan Vasilievich Is Changing Jobs (Russia)	19.7	49.9
Hard Target (USA)	19.4	59.2
On Deadly Ground (USA)	19.2	50.0
Official Romance (Russia)	18.7	52.4
Crossroads (Russia)	17.5	46.8
The Most Charming and Attractive (Russia)	17.3	41.9
Man in the Iron Mask (US-England)	16.9	44.7
Metro (USA)	16.8	46.1

Source: NTV

any other channel, with RTR in second place. Their programs are considered the most popular in every program group. Viewers' tastes change slowly, and they are inclined to preserve their old viewing patterns.

The top ten Russian television programs usually consist of films, sports, and news, with films being the most popular programs among viewers. The position of films on Russian television differs from that of soap operas and series. The Soviet Union had a strong domestic film production, and many of the old films have maintained their popularity throughout the years. Recently, Russian film production that collapsed in the early 1990s has been able to gain back its vitality. The most popular film in 1999 was a Russian film, *Peculiarities of National Hunting*, and five out of the top popular films were Russian. U.S. films such as *Pretty Woman*, *Hard Target*, and *On Deadly Ground* have received the highest ratings. The top films are mostly from the United States, because the Russian public likes Hollywood action films, especially those that are computer-animated. But the Russian viewing public also enjoys films from other countries, such as French and Indian films—the film that has gained the highest ratings on NTV is the French film *Angelica*.

Although the ratings of serials are relatively high, they seldom reach the top ten. A Russian serial, *Street of Broken Lamps*, enjoyed the highest popularity in 1999, and both ORT's and NTV's domestic serials enjoy the highest ratings of all serials. The ratings of other serials are considerably lower. The mass lure of soap operas largely faded away, and they seldom reached the top ten in 1999. Among

Table 5.6   Top Serials on Russian Television in 1999

Serial	Rating	Audience Share
Street of Broken Lamps (Russia)	19.2	53.0
Thorn Birds (US)	16.6	44.1
Eternal Call (Russia)	15.1	42.6
Cruel Angel (Latin America)	14.9	61.8
In the Name of Love (Latin America)	12.2	55.4
Delicate Poison (Latin America)	10.4	53.7
Waiting Room (Russia)	9.9	31.8
D. D. D. Detective Dubrovsky's Dossier (Russia)	9.8	31.0

Source: NTV

the top ten serials, there were four Russian serials, three from Latin America, and one from the United States. The Russian audience has lost its taste for U.S. serials, and seemingly prefers domestic and Latin American.

In the years immediately following the collapse of the Soviet Union, the Russian audience only wanted to see Western films. However, after a saturation point had been reached, a return to domestic films took place. There appeared to be nostalgia for the past. The stable, although stagnated, past may be attractive to older people in the present turbulent and insecure times. This pattern did not differ greatly from Western Europe. The results are very similar to Tomlinson's observations made on the number of U.S. television shows on European national channels (1997, 180). According to Tomlinson, it almost always turns out that: (a) it is home-produced programs that top the ratings; and (b) foreign imports generally operate at a "cultural discount" in terms of their popularity with audiences. He quotes David Morley and Kevin Robins, who write that "U.S. imports tend to do well when domestic television is not producing comparable entertainment programming—and whenever viewers have the alternative of comparable entertainment programming in their own language, the American programs tend to come off second best" (Tomlinson 1997, 181).

RESISTANCE TO THE GLOBAL

The increase in the number of foreign programs on Russian television has become a target for some Russian intellectuals and politicians, which can be seen as a form of resistance against globalization. As Ellis has observed, Soviet/Russian writers have accused late Soviet and contemporary Russian television of polluting the minds of people, particularly young people (1996, 26). Rasputin (quoted by Ellis 1999, 126) objects to what he regards as the moral permissiveness and lustfulness, the unscrupulousness and sensationalism of the mass media. Ellis writes: "Rasputin and his colleagues firmly identify this state of affairs with the influence of the Western media, particularly television-programming, radio formats, and game shows. A frequently voiced criticism is that Western media promote a materialistic outlook that is inimical to the cultural interests and growth of Russia" (1999, 126–27).

This view is not uncommon; partly it has to do with the cultural shift from written to electronic culture in Russian society. Television is an easy target in the same way as it has been in Western societies. The tone of the accusations is very similar to that in other countries when television was first introduced. As Dutkina writes: "Television plays a significant role in the growth of juvenile crimes, as does all of mass culture with its cult of violence. The mass media is an ideal mechanism for raising all sorts of maniacs, sadists, and perverts. Children playing on the Street pretend they are Freddy Krueger from *Nightmare on Elm Street,* sticking nails in their gloves for claws" (1996, 100).

The public debate about the role of national television has so far not resulted in any changes in legislation. Although there have been seven draft bills for a Broadcasting Act, only one was passed, but was ultimately not signed by President Yeltsin. The draft bill from the summer of 1997 included an article to protect national producers. The share of foreign programs on state-owned stations was to be limited to a maximum of one-third of airtime (excluding news, education, sport, and international programs) from 6 p.m. to 12 p.m. In private broadcasting, the allocation of foreign shareholdings was limited to 33 percent, but it was not specified whether existing stations were affected by this regulation (Lutz and Jankowski 1998, 64). It remains to be seen whether the draft bill will become a law.

CONCLUSION

Russian television enjoys a unique position compared to other media. No other medium is available to, and used by, so many people. As in other parts of the world, Russian television has provided the experience of globalization to ordinary people. It is through television that most people, no matter where they live, receive new global pictures into their daily life.

At the same time, Russian television has gone through a significant transformation after the collapse of Communism. The liberalization of the market has introduced new channels and new ownership forms, including mixed state-private and municipal ownership. The state affiliated (ORT, partly state-owned; RTR, wholly state-owned) channels have maintained their position and popularity among viewers in a new multichannel environment. In this sense, despite new ownership forms adopted from the West, the ownership of Russian television has maintained its own specific features. The state has remained the most important owner and controller of Russian television.

Russian television became globalized to the extent that it adopted the contents and formats of Western European and U.S. television. There are several new elements in it that support the arguments for import and modeling. Entertainization took place on every channel. Furthermore, the programs flowed mainly from the West, but not entirely, since Russians preferred soap operas that were imported from Latin America. In this sense, globalization has been a one-way street in Russia, with the collapse of Communism and state control opening the doors to the foreign import of programs.

The picture is not yet complete. In Russia, it has not been a question of global versus national television, but rather a national system absorbing global elements and transforming them into national elements. There are several examples of indigenization of global television. The dubbing of foreign programs is an example of how foreign products are made national by changing the language. The use of foreign formats for domestic programs is another example of indigenization. When global meets national, it is always a mixture of both elements, a transformation of the global into the national.

Russia is also different from other postcommunist countries because of its size. It was once part of a superpower that was able to export films and programs. Its home market is still large enough to maintain the production of indigenous programs. After the collapse of the state-supported audio-visual industry, a new domestic industry has been born. With the reservoir of old films and serials from the

Soviet period and new production of its own, post-Communist Russia is not solely dependent on imported production. What also ceased was any flow from Russia to the countries in Central and Eastern Europe, and vice versa.

Further, it is a question of the consumption patterns of the audience. The Russian audience has stayed faithful to the old channels, although it has obviously welcomed the new ones. Its most popular programs are films, especially from the United States. But about half of the top ten films are also Soviet and Russian. The audience, in Russia and elsewhere, favors domestic films if they are available. Films were always popular—even in the Soviet era they achieved the highest popularity on television (Hopkins 1970, 332). Further, they are available because the Soviet Union used to be a major film producer. The fact that the audience has discovered old domestic films after the first wave of globalization indicates that, even when societies collapse and open up to global elements that they have been deprived of, they return to domestic products if they are available. What constitutes the relationship between the global menu and the national agenda is always a question of negotiation, not only between the suppliers (global producers and national producers), but with the audience as well. And it never is an either/or question.

Monroe E. Price has written that "globalism depends not just on the reach of the producer but on the power of the State" (1995, 18). In post-Communist Russia, the state is clearly holding and, in fact, increasing its grip over television. Interestingly, it does it even without coherent legislation. In fact, the globalization of Russian television shows how the national can strike back. The resistance to globalization can be seen in structures, contents, and reception.

Finally, globalization is also a question of economy. In 1998, Russia's financial crises revealed television's vulnerability when advertising revenues were severely reduced. For example, ORT's earnings from advertising were expected to fall by as much as 50 percent, while state funding has not been forthcoming ever since the government sold off 49 percent of the company shares. NTV was considering temporary pay cuts for workers as a possible measure. CTV considered cutting the services of at least one-third of its staff ("Paper Views Effects on ORT of Advertising Crisis" 1998, 3). The option available in this situation is to fill the program time with domestic reruns and sports. The globalization of television is often about money; the domestication of television is often about the lack of it.

Could Russian television gain back the former position Soviet television had in Central and Eastern Europe, and thus bring new sources of revenues to Russian television companies? There is little interest in Central Europe, where Western programs dominate, but there are already signs that in the former Soviet republics, where Russian television programs were rejected after independence, they are regaining a foothold. This has happened in countries such as the Ukraine and Belarus, whose languages are close to Russian. Also, the Russian-speaking minorities in the Baltics have also turned to Russian television (Lutz and Jankowski 1998, 62). However, the transmission of MIR (an interstate television and radio corporation that was set up in ten out of sixteen former Soviet republics) ceased in 1997 because of low audiences—the ratings varied between 0.5 and 2 percent (Lutz and Jankowski 1998, 62).

Russia, unlike the old Soviet Union, can no longer afford to import free programs, but must establish commercial contacts. In the global trade of television programs, Russia is a newcomer that has a lot to learn.

6

Advertising

Theories about cultural globalization can roughly be divided into two categories, those of homogenization and those of heterogenization. The homogenization theories seek evidence for cultural imperialism, Westernization, dependence, and synchronization, while the heterogenization theories look for hybridization, cultural mélange, and creolization (see, for example, Pieterse 1995, 62). Advertising is often viewed as one of the negative consequences of globalization—homogenization par excellence such as McDonaldization or Coca-Colanization of the entire world. According to this view, advertising is closely connected with U.S.-style consumerism (Sklair 1995) and capitalist commodity production, and is thus a missionary of corporate capitalism (Herman and McChesney 1997). Advertising can result in negative effects on values, such as consumption as the primary way of life, displacement of the public sphere with commercialization and entertainment, and the erosion of local cultures (Herman and McChesney 1997, 154).

If we follow the argumentation of the heterogenization theorists, the intersection of the global and the local evokes a plurality of reactions to globalization. According to Featherstone, peripheral cultures can distinguish different strategies towards the mass and consumer culture images and goods originating from metropolitan centers (1995, 116). As mentioned in chapters 1 and 5, Featherstone outlines absorption/assimilation/resistance strategies in relationship to globalization. The assumption here is that cultures react in one way or

107

another, because these strategies involve activity and response. However, it is not only cultures that react, but also people who respond, in various ways, to globalization. Their response is a part of emerging cultural strategies in relation to globalization, and it is ever changing. What is absorption one day is resistance the next, and the strategies vary in different groups and subcultures of people. When Western theorists debated about the value of different cultural globalization theories, a process that changed the whole world order took place: the collapse of Communism. Curiously, it happened almost unnoticed by the globalization theorists, especially in the arena of cultural globalization. In post-Communist Russia alone, 147.7 million people who had rarely seen Western advertising were suddenly exposed to it. The change from the non-consumerist communist past to the present-day market economy was a very radical transformation indeed.

Advertising in post-Communist Russia as a form of globalization provides evidence for both homogenization and heterogenization theories. On the one hand, advertising, which was almost wholly imported to Russia, would seem to be the perfect carrier of Western values. Even the English language came with advertising to post-Communist Russia. As John Downing writes, "it (not only on TV) quite often used English as a sign of cachet, rather than Russian," and that imported Western objects frequently have foreign language texts "as a kind of guarantee of 'non-Russo-Soviet' authenticity" (1996, 132). Thus, advertising in post-Communist Russia could easily fit into the media imperialism or the homogenization globalization model. On the other hand, advertising in post-Communist Russia gives support to the heterogenization theories—how transnational corporations tailor their advertising products to specific audiences and markets, for example (Featherstone 1995, 118).

What also makes post-Communist Russia different from many societies is that, for the first time in over seventy years, Russians were able to adopt a new "global consumer identity," an identity that crossed national and political boundaries, and thus contradicts all their former identities which were based on ideology, superpower status, or nationalism. This identity was already emerging in the Communist era, although it was suppressed. After the collapse of Communism, global consumer identity replaced a former international communist identity—a sense of belonging to an international fraternity of the communist countries—of which the Soviet Union was the leader. The former international identity was thus overrun by a very different identity that did not offer a leading role in the global union of consuming nations, but a role of a newcomer with no experience and fewer resources.

Advertising in post-Communist Russia thus offers a case study through which it is possible to understand how cultural globalization works in a non-Western country. The aim of this chapter is to explore the role of advertising in post-Communist Russia as an agent of globalization. It also critically discusses the adaptability of globalization theories in a non-Western context.

ADVERTISING IN THE SOVIET UNION

Advertising is new in Russia, since it hardly existed in the Soviet Union despite the 1920s New Economic Policy (NEP) period. The estimated advertising expenditure of total household consumption was 0.03–0.07 percent in 1967. Brief announcements in the press and on television would publicize the specifications and prices of goods for sale, and the addresses of the stores where it was possible to buy these goods (McNair 1991, 87). Curiously, most goods that were advertised in the Soviet period were the ones that nobody wanted to buy. The new goods that were in strong demand often "disappeared" before they even reached the market (Hanson 1974, 50, 151). Or, as Mickiewitcz remarks, advertising was used not for the creation of needs, but rather to supplement government policy (1997, 29). If the government produced a product that did not meet public demand, it was advertised. Of course, the lack of advertising was not a separate phenomenon, but was connected to the lack of consumer goods and markets. Ferenc Feher et al. make an important observation: Communism was dictatorship over needs (1983). It was the state and the party that decided what the citizens needed. For example, such consumer goods as lipstick, condoms, maxi-pads, deodorant, razor blades, chewing gum, plastic bags, jeans, etc., that were mass produced and consumed in the West, were seldom available to average Soviet citizens, and often became familiar to them only through their contacts with foreigners. Thus, consumer goods became identified with the West, the promised land of consumer

goods. Soviet consumer goods, if they were available, came to represent poor quality and old-fashioned styles. In the Soviet republics,
such as Estonia, where it was possible to watch foreign television, the
Estonians learned about the standard of life in a capitalist country by
watching Finnish television. As Beck puts it, "television advertising,
which is often scorned by cultural criticism in the West, changed in
an environment of shortage and regimentation into a fused promise
of consumption and political freedom" (2000, 66).

One could be cynical about the need for goods like lipstick or
deodorant. But the dictatorship over needs resulted in an unsatisfied
desire for everything that was not available. As a regular visitor to
the Soviet Union, I sometimes thought that Communism could have
been rescued if consumer goods had been available. So strong was
the desire for them that carrying a Finnish plastic shopping bag
became a fashion among women in Leningrad, where Finnish tourists often went for weekend trips. Foreigners, and especially their
clothing, were keenly observed, and served as walking advertisements of what was available in the West. Western clothes became
especially important for women and youth, because the Soviet Union
did not recognize their special needs. Communism was one for all,
despite gender or age. Its uniformity made people look for a difference, to differentiate oneself from everyone else. It was not only dictatorship over needs, but dictatorship over desire.

Soviet citizens did not have a global consumer identity; instead, the
state and the Communist Party defined their needs and desires. The
lack of consumer identity is, surprisingly, closely connected with
political identity. For citizens who were denied identity as consumers,
the lack of consumer autonomy became a serious issue in a society
that also denied its citizens full political participation—their full
political identity as citizens. Graham Murdoch writes:

> The development of the modern nation-state can be read, in part, as a
> history of attempts to manage mass participation in the political proc-
> ess. These efforts have been dominated by two opposed rhetorical fig-
> ures. On the one side stood the crowd—emotional, seduced by
> dramatic images, acting in concert, bargaining by riot and demonstra-
> tion. On the other side stood citizens—rational, open to sequential
> argument, making considered personal choices, and registering prefer-
> ences soberly, in the solitude of the voting booth. (1993, 527)

Murdoch obviously writes about countries in which both voting and demonstrating are legitimate ways to express one's political identity. Both options were abstract notions in the Soviet Union. In a one-party system there were no real alternatives in voting, and riots and demonstrations, despite their canonization in the October Revolution, were not an option unless one wanted to get arrested and sent to jail. In an advanced capitalist society there is another identity available. Murdoch continues:

> Official discourse has, not surprisingly, devoted itself to advancing the responsibilities of citizenship and denigrating the seductions of the crowd. The figure of the consumer, however, presents considerable problems for this enterprise for two reasons. First, the consumer system offers personal solutions to public difficulties. It promises that it is possible to purchase peace of mind and well-being by buying a suitable commodity. In so doing, it cuts across the appeals to the public good that underpin the rhetorics of citizenship. Secondly, as early observers were quick to see, consumer markets could be viewed as "psychological crowds" in the sense that the vagaries of fashion and the advent of crazes also required immersion in the warm bath of collective action. (1993, 527)

What if, as was the case in the Soviet Union, on the one hand there was a citizen who had no real political alternatives except symbolic voting, no rights to demonstrate or riot, no religious rights, and was expected to sacrifice her or his own personal needs and desires for the common good—Communism? And on the other hand, there was a frustrated citizen who did not know how to use her or his money because there were so few consumer goods available. In this situation, there was no individual choice either in the public or in the private sphere. The collective nature of the society became totalitarian in its emphasis on rationality and common goals, leaving very little space for individualism.

The yearning for consumer goods was intimately linked to the desire for the global and, particularly, in this case, for Westernization. The Soviet Union emphasized "internationalism" in its official ideology, but it was always limited to other communist or sympathetic countries. Westernization was equivalent to capitalism, and therefore Soviet citizens had to be protected from it. The first, or official, society had a dual attitude to the West. On the one hand, the

Soviet Union was compared to the West, and if the former managed to do something better than the latter, it was considered a great achievement. On the other hand, the West was looked down on because of its false values and politics. In both cases, the relationship was far from neutral, and resulted in isolation from the West. Citizens' own society, the second society, formed its own policy, which, if not entirely opposed to the official line, was certainly critical of it. As a result, as Carl Rohde and Carsten Pellikaan write, the West did not seem to provide only "democracy" and "freedom," but far more tangible riches and consumer goods (1995, 135).

Access to the West in the Soviet period, when tourism was limited and mass media were censored, took place in indirect ways. Foreign tourists became a major source of Western consumer goods such as chewing gum or plastic bags. This was a grassroots level of globalization that already existed in the Soviet period, although in a repressed form. The second society experienced its own form of globalization that was very different from the socialist idea of internationalization. In official propaganda, the advanced West, and especially the United States, was political enemy number one, but in the second society the West came to symbolize not only wealth and access to consumer goods, but also personal freedom. As a young Kazakhstani put it, almost all people, especially the young, dreamt about visiting the United States because life there was so exciting and full of opportunities. He himself made the trip, and while in California, he fondly remembered how he first saw Sunmaid California Raisins on a cold winter evening, in a grocery shop in Almaaty, the former capital of Kazakhstan and how they made him feel warm (Nurpeissov 1998a). Raisins were available in the Soviet Union, but not in red boxes with a smiling woman on them. Sunmaid California Raisins were not only raisins, but beautifully packaged and rarely available—a symbol of a promise of a better life.

Alen Warde (1994, 878) argues that people define themselves through the messages they send to others through the goods and practices they posses and display. In the Soviet Union, Western goods became desirable because they symbolized the promised world that was denied. Earlier, almost any Western good was considered a luxury worth having, as the widely spread black market trade between tourists and locals in jeans or nylon stockings exemplified (Gronow 1997, 50). According to a survey in 1987, Soviet teenagers yearned to possess Western goods: 80 percent wanted clothing items and the rest wanted electronic equipment. Soviet consumer goods became the least desirable. Even when the Soviet Union started producing jeans, a product in great demand among young people, their quality and style never met people's standards. They had to be Western jeans, and in the mid-seventies two Italian firms were allowed to start exporting jeans into the Soviet Union. When female teenagers in Moscow were asked whether they would date young men who did not wear jeans, the majority said no (Shlapentokh 1989, 151). A young man describes how he and his fellow students found Italian jeans that were not available in Moscow in a small village 150 kilometers from Moscow in 1984. His story also reveals how expensive jeans were compared to food at that time:

> We went to a small village shop and to our amazement they had a stock of Italian "Riffle" jeans, a highly desirable item among young people, at a price of eighty-five rubles. But there was a precondition: you first had to give one hundred eggs to the shop to buy them. So we first bought the eggs from the very same shop at a price of 1.2 rubles, and then gave them back to the shop and bought the jeans. (Nurpeissov 2000)

The popularity of jeans increased the awareness of style. Particularly in the trade in jeans between tourists and Soviet citizens, the trademark, such as Levis, became more and more important. This consumer consciousness developed entirely in the second society, because officially these items were not promoted and were scarcely available. Soviet citizens saw no advertisements but developed their taste mainly by watching tourists.

The *Perestroika* of Advertising

Nancy Condee and Vladimir Padunov list among the first signs of the new epoch the t-shirts that appeared in the mid-perestroika years (1987–89) satirizing Lenin by juxtaposing him with the major commercial icons of U.S. capitalism—first Lenin and Coca-Cola, Lenin under the Golden Arches of McDonald's, then Lenin reading *Pravda* beside two bottles of Pepsi (1985, 132). According to these authors, these pictures were meant to strike an ironic stance toward capitalism but, in fact, advertised these goods. But soon, "real" Russian advertising—in the form of plastic bags—appeared. Condee and Padunov write:

> Out on the street, socialism's faux-leather briefcase, filled with canned goods and sausage, and its string-bags, topped with radishes and dill weed, have ceded their primacy to the commercial plastic bag (*paketik*), advertising Trekhgornaia manufaktura (Three-Hills Manufacturing Company) or Gzhel's porcelain. The commercial plastic bags differ from socialism's thick, cloudy plastic bags, stamped with imitation woodcarving motifs in bile green or baby blue. The new *paketiki* are products of a different market, their physical and aesthetic desirability is inextricably linked with their advertising function. They not only are something, they do something: they suggest what to buy next. (1995, 131)

Citizens found their own way to demonstrate the change made by *perestroika*—by carrying plastic bags for the first time made in Russia and advertising Russian companies. It is important to note that this was something that was not produced from above, but was a person's own way to express his or her changing identity from Soviet citizens to potential consumers. In this way, people became media before the new advertising media were born. Carrying plastic bags or wearing Western clothes symbolized a promise about something that was about to emerge—a change in the existing society. Advertising, at this point, was not something that was imported on a large scale—it was people taking foreign items into use or making them themselves.

Gradually, advertising became a more mass-produced phenomenon. A visible sign in big cities was the appearance of billboards. One cannot overestimate the visibility of the change when new brand names and billboards appeared in Moscow. In the early days of *perestroika,* most of the billboards were in English—the first time that English was publicly used. Only later did the authorities decide that the Russian language should also be used in public advertisements. The signs of McDonald's, Pizza Hut, Coke, or Marlboro were suddenly announcing not only that new consumer goods were available on a mass scale, but also that the closed society was opening up. There was a lot of excitement about these visible changes, and people queued to have their first hamburgers in the newly opened McDonald's restaurants. Private kiosks started selling Western alcohol, chocolate, and cigarettes. Almost everybody could buy a piece of globalization.

Most of the things that were advertised were also available at a relatively low price, such as sweets, chewing gum, or shampoo. These were, of course, products that were not available before. The new scents, colors, and packaging materials were intoxicating for people who did not have these products before. Advertising became the most globalizing element in people's everyday life because it was present not only in images, but also in goods that could be smelled, touched, and consumed if bought: the West had arrived in people's daily life. However, there was a controversy between desire and affordability. Galina Dutkina describes her visit to GUM, the former State Department Store, after the introduction of the market economy:

> Karlstadt, Reebok, Adidas, Salamander. Shoes, men's clothing (usually just suit jackets and raincoats). Eyeglasses and Italian pizza. Coca-Cola. After about ten minutes my head began to ache. A particularly vivid impression remains from the housewares department, where brass bathroom fixtures cost $120 and curtain rods went for $230. Given the minimum monthly Russian salary of $9, and even the average salary of $110, the prices were unbelievable. But this is just the tip of the iceberg. (1996, 8–9)

Advertising and Mass Media

In addition to the globalization of urban space, advertising started to change the economy, structure, and contents of the old media. Soviet viewers had seen their first television advertisements in 1987 when U.S. commercials appeared during the live broadcast—"Capital to Capital"—of the satellite *Space Bridge* on Soviet television and ABC. The first advertisements for Soviet private firms appeared in the press and on television after 1985, when the Communist Party started to encourage their establishment (McNair 1991, 87). Following the appearance of the television program *Vzglyad* (*Viewpoint*) in 1987, many television schedules began placing a commercial between various program segments. Companies were allowed to advertise on Soviet television for the rate of seventy-eight rubles per minute in the Moscow region (McNair 1991, 87).

Television, radio, and newspapers gradually became full of advertisements. New glossy magazines such as *Marie Claire, Vogue,* and *Elle* were published with whole page advertisements never before seen. A new identity was about to be born: a consumer's identity of access to global goods that were available around the world, even in Russia. This new identity was a global identity; it connected post-Communist Russia with the rest of the world. Finally, after decades of suppressed desires, global consumerism was reflected in the form of advertising. And gradually, more and more consumer goods became available. Advertising was experienced as if Russia had finally become similar to every other nation joining a global league of consumerist nations.

In the beginning, Russian consumers embraced advertising because it was novel—something that did not exist before. Advertising opened a window to the beauty of things that were not necessarily even for sale, but could be admired. A foreign advertiser complained that "Russian consumers want everything they have been deprived of and they want it now. That is why there is a lot of glamour. But then you get the problem with the consumer watching the background and not the product. We are trying to sell furniture polish but everyone is admiring the table" (Philips 1995).

In 1991 advertising expenditures totaled only $3 million, but started to rise rapidly as table 6.1 shows. However, in Russia, the amount per inhabitant spent on advertising (twelve dollars) is still the lowest in Europe ("Sredstva massovoi informatsii Rossii" 1998, 144,146)

Although in the late 1980s Soviet cooperatives had already started to advertise their products, mass-market advertising, be it on billboards or in media, was initially imported. Unlike other forms of media and communications in post-Communist Russia, early mass-advertising was mainly foreign owned. There was no law on advertis-

Table 6.1   Development of Advertising in Russia

Channel	1998			1999		
	Number	*Seconds*	*US$*	*Number*	*Seconds*	*US$*
ORT	119,354	2,614,264	1,127,325,801	95,003	1,950,298	873,325,024
RTR	60,772	1,410,546	453,310,485	104,780	2,251,896	545,232,682
TVC	60,851	1,398,780	119,615,474	67,372	1,397,029	88,826,024
NTV	80,278	1,733,917	495,025,546	127,748	2,380,365	617,516,278

Source: Russian Public Relations Group.

ing that would have prevented foreign ownership, and most firms started as branch offices of big global companies. In February 1989, Ogilvy & Mather became the first officially registered Western advertisement agency in the Soviet Union by forming a joint venture with the Soviet *Soyztorgreklama* and Hungary's *Mahir* (McKay and Gutterman 1994). In the beginning of the 1990s, several global advertising agencies, such as Young & Rubican and BBDO, opened branch offices in Moscow. The foreign agencies are still the biggest: DMB&B (US$ 57.6 million), Ogilvy & Mather (US$ 30.9 million), and BBDO Marketing (US$ 28.1 million). The products these companies advertise also dominate the advertising space across different media. For example, on television foreign advertisers account for 50 percent of advertising time and 65 percent of expenditures ("Sredstva massovoi informatsii Rossii" 1998, 164, 176).

The appearance of advertising in the media completely changed its economy and content. The media now had to take into account two new factors previously nonexistent in the Soviet era: audiences and advertisers. They now had to compete against each other not only for audiences, but also for advertising money. The results became similar to those in many other countries—the media started to resemble each other. The different television stations showed similar soap operas and serials because it was the safest way to attract a high number of viewers to bring in more advertising money. It was not only the contents of different media that became more homogenized, but also advertising itself—different media advertised the same products. The change in newspapers or magazines was strikingly visible; often the paper was imported, and the printing was done outside the country. As a result, the new magazines bore only a slight resemblance to the old thick, brown, and colorless Soviet magazines. The fact that new advertising was imported, although carried partly by the old media, such as television or newspapers, brought the new into the old and changed it profoundly.

The Social Use of Advertising

Although the early response to advertising was overwhelmingly positive, critical voices began to be heard, and the spate of foreign advertisements created a counterresponse. Complaints about *snickerizatsiya* (Snickersization) of the economy were raised after the U.S.-

Table 6.2 Most Prominent Foreign Advertisers on Russian Television

Advertiser	1999				1998			
	Advertisements	Airtime (seconds)	US$	Rating	Advertisements	Airtime (seconds)	US$	Rating
Procter & Gamble	30,661	953,253	298,251,027	1	64,778	2,295,848	497,498,681	1
Nestle	22,197	534,651	169,109,862	2	20,978	531,951	151,168,660	3
Mars Rossiia	25,834	566,881	130,637,591	3	21,185	554,640	124,871,426	4
Unilever	17,516	419,915	88,922,732	4	24,157	664,097	175,570,802	2
Wrigley	27,166	495,525	87,869,864	5	27,816	585,916	108,783,225	5
Dandy	23,155	437,574	80,526,212	6	31,658	530,732	107,487,607	6
Pepsi Co.	16,840	386,630	56,169,165	7	10,130	255,891	51,932,976	10
Coca-Cola	12,065	302,845	54,247,714	8	11,822	363,968	65,738,001	9
L'Oreal	3,373	81,673	38,830,285	9	3,545	77,977	40,475,176	11
Danone	8,071	126,690	32,233,550	10	1,525	24,029	11,544,028	20

Source: Russian Public Relations Group

based Mars group flooded the country with its Snickers bars in the early 1990s and filled the airwaves with its advertisements (Thornhill 1995). This was a huge campaign directed to Russian consumers, not only to increase their awareness of the availability of Western chocolate, but also even to change their consumption habits and taste. Russian consumers who had earlier identified their domestic dark chocolate with dessert were now introduced to new milk chocolate that was to be consumed as snacks. Despite the huge campaign, it was difficult to completely change people's habits, even though Mars and other chocolate bars are now widely consumed. As Dutkina writes:

> There were two shelves of imported ice cream and chocolate bars, objects of lust for all Russian kids—Bounty, Snickers, Mars, Milky Way, Twix, and others. Thanks to some clever television advertising, in the last years these brands have completely squeezed Russian chocolate out of the market. In relation to the minimum wages and even the average wage—these candy bars are very expensive, particularly in the brand name stores. (1996, 15)

There were also, however, advertising campaigns that failed. The most well known is "Your Cat Would Buy Whiskas" and "Wash & Go." According to Kelly, the former suggests that the cat is the only member of the household who could be naïve enough to waste money on that stuff (1988, 228). The cat food advertisement resulted in anti-advertising sentiments, especially after a reader's letter to a newspaper from a retired man who asked where he could buy this highly nutritious food for himself. Many people found it repulsive that special cat food was advertised in a situation where millions of people were living below the poverty line.

The shampoo and conditioner advertisement "Wash & Go" was based on the assumption that Russian women, like their Western counterparts, are too busy to find time to use both shampoo and conditioner. The message of "Wash & Go," where two processes are combined in one, giving more time for other activities, was based on the image of a busy Western lifestyle. The Western advertisement showing a woman leaving the gym before others did not appeal to female Russian viewers, and the campaign had to be relaunched. As a manager of a Russian advertising agency put it, "the ad campaign reflected a typical Western lifestyle and the message was not appropriate" (Philips 1995). Also, as Kelly observes, its authors failed to realize that the Russian word for conditioner is, in fact, "balsam"; what they were actually advertising was shampoo with a built-in hair conditioner (1998, 223–24). The Mars and Snickers advertisements were also not very popular on Russian television, mainly due to their tiresome repetition of a phrase from the television commercial, 'Tolstyi, tolstyi sloi shokolada' (Thick, very thick layer of chocolate), which became a popular expression in Russia for something notoriously boring.

One of the lessons Western advertisers learned in post-Communist Russia was that advertisements had to be nationalized to attract Russian consumers. Although foreign companies still spend considerably more on advertising than Russian companies, global advertising companies had to admit that they did not know enough about Russian culture to produce advertisements for Russian audiences. The emergence of Russian advertising agencies has introduced a partial domestication of the advertising market. In 1998, there were 2,000 domestic advertising agencies in Moscow and 5,000 in the whole country. In the late 1990s, the profits of the biggest domestic advertising agencies have started to exceed the profits of their foreign counterparts in Russia—Video International, with a $32 million profit, and Maksima with $40 million ("Sredstva massovoi informatsii Rossii" 1998, 163). Increasingly, foreign clients also use Russian firms to design their campaigns. The latter know the taste of their consumers better, and thus can avoid the mistakes foreign advertisers have made in the past. Russian companies have rapidly learned the know-how of the new field.

There have been clear signs of counterreactions, and a turn to domestic advertisements, much in the same way as Russians reacted to foreign films and serials. One of the most successful Russian television commercials in 1999 was for *Staryi Melnik* (Old Miller) beer. Russian beer is something deeply national, and drinking domestic beer that promises a bright future was shown in another successful commercial for beer, the *Zolotaya bochka* (Golden Barrel) brand. This commercial starts with a picture of a group of young men in their early thirties. They are lying in the sand in a depressed mood. Then one of them notices a bottle of beer in the sand. They begin to drink it, and the camera widens its picture to reveal that they are actually lying on sand in an open railroad car on a moving train. The slogan of the commercial is "Pivo Zolotaya Bochka —Nado Chasche Vstrechatsia" (The Golden Barrel Beer —Need to Meet More Often) (Evstafiev 2000).

Tensions between the Old and the New

The introduction of advertising has been undoubtedly the most globalizing element in Russian everyday life. Ordinary people welcomed it with open arms, because it was new, exciting, and available to everybody. However, the development of the market economy and the division of Russian society into "haves" and "have-nots" have changed the situation. Advertising reflects the growing rift in Russian society between the "haves," who have embraced the whole arena of advertising and capitalist culture with less critical facility than in the West, and the "have-nots," the low-income people who remain "very traditional and anti-advertising" (Gutterman 1994). The images of consumer goods that cannot be afforded, but can be identified with the West, do not only divide Russian society but also increase awareness of the difference between the West and Russia. Even in the case of sweets and other relatively inexpensive products, 50 percent of consumers cannot afford anything of the advertised consumer goods, 40 percent might buy an imported shampoo or chocolate bar, and 10 percent have real disposable income ("Better Data" 1995). Of course, in the Russian context, 50 percent translates to over 70 million people, but at the same time, there is the other half that can only watch, rather than buy.

The high tide of Westernization occurred in the early 1990s— immediately after the old system collapsed, when everything had to be Westernized, and there was no opposition to it; old values were rejected, especially by young people (Neumann 1996, 168). According to a survey, practically all young people (approximately 97 percent) showed a negative attitude toward communism and socialism as values in the period of 1992–1994 (Riordan et al. 1995, 21). It was also a time when people felt grief and disappointment over their former Soviet past. Elena Gourko writes:

> Now, we are lost and disappointed. When we feel ourselves as a people to be second rate, when we are sad and angry, a lot of Russians, maybe

the majority, are thinking, that it was a great misfortune to be born here, in a former "Communist paradise," to speak Russian (or any other language of the Soviet Union), which is useless for communications outside the country, and in general, (a great misfortune) to be Russians or Soviets, citizens of a former "superstate," which now is asking the international community for urgent help, food, and money. Russians, who are considered to be a great nation with ancient and rich culture are often ashamed of being Russians, since practically everything marked by the definitions "Russian" appears to be now not reasonable, not modern or good enough. So, no surprise, that everything of that kind is sharply criticized and often totally rejected by young people, who are more free-minded and energetic than others. I would like to stress once again, that such a rejection is a rejection not only of our "Communist past," but more and more often of our "Russian present" and "Russianness" in general; it was proved, besides other reasons, by the emigration from the USSR, grown as a snowball together with the advancement of *perestroika*. (1993, 60–61)

Since consumer desires had been suppressed for half a century, and "Russian" was considered not modern or good enough, the appetite for the West knew no limits. The new unrestricted access made Western-style consumption possible for the first time. Gradually, however, the emerging, peculiarly Russian market economy hit back. The early years of *perestroika* were full of the promise of change, something that would be full of opportunities, something better than the old. The transition from the old to the new became much more difficult for most people than they could have ever imagined. In 1991 consumer prices suddenly started to increase. The price of bread, which had remained at twenty-four kopecks for more than twenty years, was raised to thirty rubles. The average Soviet monthly salary was up to 120 rubles, the equivalent of twenty-five dollars; and twenty-five kopecks was equal to ten cents. Inflation reached 2,984 percent (Nurpeissov 1998b). Between 1991 and December 1996, consumer prices increased 1,700 times. Low-income earners account for around a third of the population (between 44 and 50 million people). Around 55 million people have fallen into poverty since the transition to the market economy (Gray 1998, 147).

Advertising is much more directly connected to consumption than, for example, films or serials. It promotes consumer goods that are available only if you can afford them. The emergence of the consumer market made advertising possible (you could actually buy the goods that were advertised), but at the same time, it made people much more aware of what was not available to them. The experience of global consumerism in a Russian context is elegantly satirized in an article entitled "Advertising Dream," published by A. Mashin in one of Moscow's regional newspapers, *Krasnaia Presnia:*

> I left the privatised enterprise and bought Snickers, Mars and Stimorol in a supermarket. I got in my own Jeep and suppressed my hunger with a chocolate bar. Then I lay back in the seat of my car and lighted up (a) Camel. After finishing my cigarette I started driving, chewing Stimorol. As I came to my house I switched on (my) Sony, and using my money-counting machine, I counted the dividends (that) I received from my shares. "Not a bad amount," I thought. "However, money should not be idle, it should be invested. It is time to think about purchasing a real estate somewhere in Santa-Barbara." I opened a can of Whiskas for my cat and offered Pedigreepal to my dog. The dog yelped with joy.
>
> I woke up. . . . I need to exchange empty bottles for money and buy a package of coarse tobacco in a bazaar. (quoted in Feofanov 2000, 50–51)

Advertising also produces an unexpected and unsettling experience—an awareness of the difference between the West and Russia. This, in turn, can either contribute to an increased sense of nationalism or to an increased sense of the global. In the first case, global elements are rejected and there is a turn to nationalist values and increasing criticism of the West. In the latter case, it is Russia that is being rejected, as in Gourko's statement. In present-day Russia, both reactions are evident.

The disappointment doubled when being able to vote did not bring the anticipated "good life." Nothing changed overnight. Life became, in many respects, more difficult with new individual, instead of collective, responsibilities. As Kolesnik observes, "The large-scale unavailability of consumer goods makes it impossible to speak of advertising geared toward the mass consumer. Instead, the consumer has been transformed into a guest at a stranger's party, who is only left to watch how joint ventures and factories spend hard currency or solve their problems with the help of barter agreements" (1991, 54).

Constant reminders of the differences between the West and Russia stimulate strategies of alienation and resistance, even a voluntary re-closing of society from the outside world. As Rohde and Pellikaan observe, in the end, advertising may produce an inimical attitude toward the West, which promises so much and gives so little (1995, 135–36). They write further about the deep crisis of legitimacy Eastern European countries are suffering:

> Trying to overcome it, people are torn between embracing the charismatic legitimacy of the "new" things that the West has to offer, and attempting to reach back to the traditional legitimacy of their own roots. Advertising plays a major role in this balancing act. During the last few years the attractiveness of this new charismatic appeal can be called almost overwhelming, and advertising was the main stimulus in that process. In the future years, however, it is not improbable that we will have to reckon with a reaction against this enthusiasm for the new and its charismatic appeal—and advertising probably will also play a significant role in those developing trends. (1995, 135)

Advertising, more than any other medium, old or new, in post-Communist Russia, promises Russians a share in globalization by building a new global consumer identity, which was prohibited in the Communist era. Advertising has become one of the most important ways for Russians to express and share global consumer identity, a sense of being part of the same world as Westerners. However, because most people's choices as consumers are limited by economic realities, advertising has become for many people a form of surrogate participation in globalization.

CONCLUSION

Neither heterogenization nor homogenization theories are adequate as such for our understanding of the specific circumstances of cultural globalization in post-Communist Russia—a unique situation, considering the size and status of the former superpower that changed rapidly from Communism to the market economy. It is a transformation that touches every aspect of life—political, economic, and cultural, and results in an identity crisis that concerns every citizen in one way or another.

Moreover, this attitude can lead to resistance identities in the form of nationalism and hostility towards the West that "promises so much but gives so little." Hence, advertising also intensifies the sense of the national. The national, at its worst, is conservative, repressive, and self-closing. At its best, the national gives people back their self-respect in the turbulent times when everything people believed in seems to have lost its meaning, and they are exposed to new images about advanced Western societies and lifestyle. There is a very thin line between these two differences—what is a radical or conservative strategy in a specific historical situation is sometimes very hard to tell.

Advertising has profoundly changed the media economy. It is present everywhere, no matter what the ownership form of a medium is. All media are increasingly dependent on advertising when state funding has dropped substantially. Advertising has homogenized the contents of different media; different Russian television channels, for example, resemble each other both in their supply of programs and in their advertisements. The same companies, the biggest of them Western, advertise in all media. In this sense, advertising in post-Communist Russia supports the view that entertainment erodes the public sphere. At the same time, it has made possible the establishment of alternative media to the old state-controlled media. NTV, the privately owned and funded television company, was largely considered the most critical in its views about the Russian government and the war in Chechnya. Thus, advertising has also contributed in creating a new public sphere.

In the Communist period, Western goods were advertisements, because no foreign advertising was permitted. At that time, they served a political function, far from the pacification function consumerism is considered to have by homogenization theorists in the Western countries. This is again an example of the variety of functions of media in different cultures. Later, the newly-born Russian consumers developed new strategies in their relationship to advertising. Advertising was first received uncritically, thus giving support to the homogenization theories about its overwhelming influence on people. Consumerism was equated with democracy, freedom to choose, and it was not questioned. In the early days of post-Communism, the difference between the Russian reality and the Western standard of life that advertising transmitted had an impact on Russian self-confidence—nothing that was Russian was considered good enough. Increasingly, however, the influence of advertising has been the opposite. It has also resulted in anti-advertising sentiments when people have become aware of the difference between advertised goods and what they can afford. In this sense, advertising produces an unpredicted critical attitude, not only towards itself, but also towards the system that cannot provide people with a standard of life that would enable them to buy some of the goods that are advertised. Hence, advertising also produces criticism and opposition.

In the Soviet Union, people lacked both political and consumer identity. The lack of these identities led to increasing dissatisfaction with their political system—a system that did not offer any choices either to voters or consumers. After the collapse of Communism, Russian people embraced and, enthusiastically, exercised their new opportunities to choose either their political candidates or the brands they were buying. However, neither of these choices brought long-term solutions into people's daily lives, which remain, for many, a struggle for existence. Gradually, people started losing interest in using their political rights because of the difficulties in their daily lives and their disillusion with politics. What many people wanted was, above all, stability in turbulent times. As a result, they have found themselves in a situation in which their political rights have been partly taken over by the government in the name of law and order. Their consumer rights are still untouched since the collapse of Communism, but they are limited by what people can afford. This time their rights as consumers are not only controlled by the government but by something that is even further beyond their control—global market forces. It will be interesting to see whether their own government or global market forces will be the primary object of Russian people's criticism.

7

Conclusion

When I was writing this book and mentioned my tentative title to people, many of them started laughing and said, "Is there such a thing as globalization in post-Communist Russia?" Some went even further, and expressed their doubts about whether the country had any media or communications to speak of. Sheer ignorance aside, a very serious question emerged: Does it matter to the rest of the world what takes place in post-Communist Russia? Why should it interest us?

According to Anthony Giddens, globalization today is only partly about Westernization. He writes: "Globalization is becoming increasingly *decentred,* not under the control of any group of nations, still less of the larger corporations. Its effects are felt as much in Western countries as elsewhere" (cited in Curran and Park 2000, 7). The "elsewhereness" as a form of decentralized globalization is exactly the reason why countries like post-Communist Russia should be studied, not only because Russia is different from other countries, but because the investigation should also change our ideas about globalization. Loren Graham has pointed out the significance of countries such as post-Communist Russia to our general understanding in the field of science and technology (1996, 126). He ends his book by asking, "What have we learned about science and technology from the Russian experience?" His guess is that some of his readers will say: I have learned a lot more about Russia than I have about science and technology. The Russian experience is so unusual that it does not tell us much about science and technology. Graham writes that such a conclusion would be a serious mistake, because it is based on two erroneous assumptions: (1) that science and technology can be separated from their societal context; and (2) that "real" science and technology can be found only in North America and Western Europe.

Graham's argument can easily be extended to the role of media and communications in globalization. First, the role of media and communications cannot be separated from their societal context; second, the "real" globalization of media and communications cannot be based only in North America and Western Europe. Western scholarship on media and communications is largely based on its false assumption of universality—how media and communications operate everywhere in a similar way. Concomitantly, since the whole concept of globalization is so tightly connected with media and communications, what follows is that globalization cannot be separated from its societal, or rather, from its national context.

Doing research on the role of media and communications in globalization is like trying to sit on at least two chairs at the same time. While many globalization theorists have referred to media and communications in trying to point out the drastic change globalization has on people, many media scholars have done almost the opposite. Increasingly, new books and articles appear in media studies that basically question the whole concept of globalization by underlining the significance of national media systems (see, for example, Curran and Park 2000; Wang et. al 2000), or by arguing that globalization is nothing more than media imperialism or Americanization or consumerism (see, for example, Boyd-Barrett 1998; Sparks 1998; Sklair 1995). As a media scholar, I can sympathize with the necessity of doing research on media itself before making generalizations on their role in globalization. At the same time, I believe that while my colleagues have been doing it, many of them have missed the big picture of globalization. What I find important is to do research on the role of media and communication in the process of globalization, and acknowledge that these two phenomena are deeply interdependent. You cannot have one without the other, and they influence each other. The more we learn about media and communications, the more we know about globalization and how it works.

When we add to this the importance of doing research on globalization in non-Western countries, there are even more chairs to sit on. Rather than trying to sit on all of the chairs at once, I find it easier to separate them out and sit on one chair at a time. At the end, I can again bring them together. In this chapter, I first analyze the role of media and communications in post-Communist Russia. Second, I consider the impact of globalization on post-Communist Russia. Third, I consider the evidence provided by post-Communist Russia on media and communications theories. Fourth, I discuss the evidence provided by the Russian case on globalization theories.

MEDIA AND COMMUNICATIONS AS AGENTS OF GLOBALIZATION IN POST-COMMUNIST RUSSIA

This book started with the need to redefine the concept of globalization when doing research on media in postcommunist societies—in this case, Russia. Russia differs from other postcommunist countries because of its sheer size and former status—an additional reason why post-Communist Russia should be studied, since it is still one of the biggest and most powerful countries in the world. However, postcommunist media in Russia bears resemblance to other Central and Eastern European countries; like CEE countries, it has encountered a flow of imported Western programs and advertisements. Unlike the CEE countries, foreign companies in Russia do not own a significant part of the national media. In the Russian case, we talk about the globalization of content, format, structures, and consumption, but not of ownership.

In this sense, Russia and other postcommunist countries were not any different from small, advanced Western countries that import most of their programs, along with the necessary structure and technology. What makes Russia and other postcommunist countries different is their recent transition from communism toward capitalism. It has been important to analyze the specific historic circumstances that have preceded the present situation, one of which is the authoritarian state and Communist Party control that lasted more than seventy years.

In postcommunist countries in general, and in Russia, in particular, it is impossible to ignore the role the state and Communist parties

played before the collapse of Communism. Although there were substantial differences between the media systems of different communist countries (Sparks 2000b, 40), the control exercised by the state
and the Party in the Soviet Union left long-lasting marks on the mediascape. In present-day Russia, the control of the media by the state
can be traced back as far as Imperial Russia. I do agree with Sparks
that party and state control have been overemphasized and thus
overpoliticized (2000b, 37), but I disagree with his notion that there
is no fundamental distinction between economic effects on the
media, derived from ownership patterns, and political effects on
media, derived from the action of governmental or state structures.

The Soviet media successfully kept citizens away from the Western
world and thus delayed the effects of globalization that were already
taking place in many parts of the world. In this sense, political factors
are very different from economic interests that, in general, push for
globalization in the pursuit of profits. This is why I think, in contrast
to Sparks, that it is important to distinguish between the political factors and the economic interests that can affect the media. Political
factors and their consequences made the Soviet Union very different
from advanced Western countries, where globalization was not coun-
tered for political reasons. As a consequence of its isolation, the
Soviet system probably survived longer than it would have in other
circumstances. The Soviet Union remained one of the last fortresses
against globalization, not only because of its huge military machine,
but also because of its relatively advanced media system that insulated it from the Western world.

However, even that massive media system could not prevent citizens' own connections with the Western world. As Ganley (1992)
puts it, personal media have explosive political power in circumstances where their users do not have it otherwise. These small, personal media or communications, as they have been called in this
book, such as tape or video recorders, were going to have an effect
no one could foresee at that time. Personal media and communications were considered insignificant compared to the big media owned
by the state and controlled by the party. However, people used these
media and communications socially in their own networks that
crossed the boundaries of the state. At the same time, the media and
communications used socially also prepared the ground for change:
people who were involved with personal communications were the

ones who had the skills to start something new when the system collapsed. Further, media and communications formed an important part of the second private economy that taught people the ABCs of capitalism in the shadow of state economy. Finally, and crucially, in the second society, they not only were used for making money, but they also helped give birth to civil society under Communism.

National media and communications systems are not monolithic entities, each with equal power. Even the Soviet media system that was once considered so powerful had its communications subsystems that developed independently. These subsystems are very important for globalization, which does not necessarily come only from above—from the big, government-controlled media—but also from below, through small media and communications. This is what happened in the Soviet Union, where small media and communications first started to import global elements into Soviet society. These elements included pop music, films, and advertising—objects of cultural criticism in the West. What is interesting and neglected is how these elements serve a different function in a closed society such as the Soviet Union. The consumption of Western mass culture became a form of resistance because it was controlled, and sometimes even sanctioned, by Soviet society. What follows from this is that although media and communications are important as such (for example, as a form of technology), what is even more important is their social use. It is people who bring meaning into the messages they hear or see— and these meanings can change. Hence, for example, advertising had a very different social function in the Soviet era compared to today.

The collapse of the Soviet system, including its mass media system, changed the position of small media and communications. Suddenly, people who had acquired their skills illegally in the second market were in big demand in the new emerging economy. Personal media and communications became not only important for people but for new enterprises. What was earlier forbidden and suppressed became open and accepted. Every radio station played Western pop music and every television channel showed Western films. With the rapid increase of imported media contents, globalization lost its political oppositional position and achieved, at some point, an almost dominant position. In the early 1990s, the globalized elements in the media were so strong that Westernization or even media imperialism concepts could have been easily used to describe the situation.

However, too much globalization is bound to cause counterreactions, mostly in the form of increasing nationalism. In a situation where a nation-state is being established at the same time it is opening up to globalization, there is a tendency to go to either of two extremes. Globalization causes increasing nationalism if people, or the state, start to become aware that globalization is becoming dominant. In post-Communist Russia, where almost all the former structures were falling apart, and people had lost their faith in Communism, imported media contents did not eventually provide them with what they needed. The disparity between reality and pictures in the media became almost too poignant and unbearable. Globalization is not necessarily a promise of something better for the future, but a threat to new life that people are trying to build.

As we see in table 7.1, there have been different stages in the globalization of media and communications in late Soviet Union and post-Communist Russia. It is important to note that globalization does not take place at once, but affects different media and communications unevenly. In general, new communications technology is more open to globalization than the old, partly because the state and the party controlled the old media. However, after the collapse of Communism, every medium and form of communications was open

Table 7.1   Different Stages of Globalization in Media and Communications in Late Soviet and Post-Communist Russia

STAGE 1: Emerging Globalization	STAGE 2: Increasing Globalization	STAGE 3: Declining Globalization
1. Emerging globalization of contents (illegal videotapes and music cassettes)	1. Rapidly increasing globalization of contents in every medium	1. Emerging nationalization of contents
2. Emerging globalization of technology imported, often illegally (tape recorders, video cassette players, faxes, etc.)	2. Emergence of new global media (advertising, new communications technology, satellite channels, etc.)	2. Merger of old and new media
3. Emerging consumption of global media products	3. Increasing markets of communications technology	3. Emerging difference in access to media and communications technology
	4. Sharp increase in the consumption of global media products	4. Partial turn to national products in consumption
		5. Emerging criticism of global media products

to globalization, and whether it was new or old, state- or privately owned, did not matter. This was a period that posed very little resistance to globalization. Inevitably, a saturation point was reached, and there was growing criticism against globalization and a partial return to national values. This was also a point when the old media regained some of their status and were able to increase their indigenous production.

In this situation, national media systems play an important role. Although their contents may be almost entirely imported, as in the case of television, national media systems still indigenize the contents. This can be done in several ways, as I have previously pointed out, but language is one of the most important factors in this process. National media systems still "speak" national languages, not only by employing these languages, but also by providing a framework that is based on the concept of "imagined community" of a nation-state.

What I have hopefully convincingly shown is that the Russian media system consists of different layers, of the old and the new media and communications. Those that are old are less apt to change, because inherited organizational structures have turned out to be very difficult to loosen. Here I can refer to both state-owned news agencies and state-controlled television. Only the new media and communications can start from a "clean table," although even they have to take into consideration the existing structures. The Internet is a good example because of its reliance on working telephone lines. It is interesting that different Russian television stations, despite their ownership forms, relied, at least in the early phase, on imported programs. Since this is a global phenomenon (excluding, of course, the United States and Great Britain), we can draw at least two conclusions. First, television as a cultural form is a global medium whose distinctive feature is imported contents. Second, following the arguments of media imperialists and homogenization theorists, we can argue that television is particularly sensitive to globalization and gives up its own nationally specific features easier than other forms of communication, such as state-owned news agencies. Here we can refer to Appadurai's concepts of soft and hard cultural forms. Obviously, television is a soft cultural form compared to state-owned news agencies.

Russia also differs from other postcommunist countries in that previously, it exported cultural products to other communist countries. This also makes it easier to fight back, because there is a reservoir of indigenous cultural products. However, never before had a communist media superpower collapsed in the way the Soviet Union did. If we define globalization only as the export and import of programs, post-Communist Russia has definitely lost the position the Soviet Union had. There are so far no contra or reverse flows: present-day Russia is almost entirely an importer with very little reciprocity. Although there is a potential market in the territories of the former Soviet Union for expatriates and Russian speakers, this niche market has not been exploited. Post-Communist Russia simply does not have the resources Great Britain or the United States have in the production of media products (Tunstall and Machin 1999).

THE IMPACT OF GLOBALIZATION ON POST-COMMUNIST RUSSIA

We cannot underestimate the impact of media and communications in the globalization of post-Communist Russia, especially if we talk about globalization as experienced in the Giddensian way. For most Russian people, especially outside big cities, globalization is experienced mainly through media. There is a growing disparity between people's access to media and communications, but by and large, television is the medium that reaches most Russian households. In a way, the Soviet Union was digging its own grave by extending its networks of media and communications. What was thought to serve the Soviet system actually prepared the ground for its collapse. Now, through television, global images are present in Russian homes. The media wall that once separated the country from the Western world is gone. Russians can experience the compression of time and space—they are no longer separated from the rest of the world.

Simultaneously, the Russian media system has changed dramatically. It is widely recognized that it has changed for good. The globalization of Russian media is there to stay, and it is highly unlikely that the country could go back to the Communist era when the state owned and the party controlled the media. The variety of different media and communications, the availability of personal media, and the presence of global media in Russia prevent turning the clocks back.

I have deliberately tried to avoid overpoliticization in my analysis by taking a point of view that stresses the media themselves. However, it is impossible not to pay attention to the incidents that took place before Yeltsin's retirement, and in the early phase of Putin's presidency in 1999–2001—the raid on the offices of Media-Most holding company (one of the companies that has benefited most from globalization); the arrest of Vladimir Gusinsky, the head of the company, on suspicion of fraud; his exile, the closure of some of his papers, and the growing pressure from the state gas monopoly Gazprom on Media-Most.

It is no coincidence that Media-Most has been under so much pressure. It was Media-Most news organizations that critically covered Russia's war in Chechnya and alleged corruption in the Kremlin. Journalists and the owners of media companies are now accused of misusing their freedom. President Putin has warned that unarmed business magnates were trying to blackmail the state. Putin said: "The State has a cudgel in its hands that you use to hit just once, but on the head. We haven't used this cudgel, yet. We've just brandished it" (Jack and Ostrovsky 2000). Putin's attack on Russian media raises questions about the role of increasing state control over Russian media. Authoritarian state control has survived from Imperial Russia, through the Soviet Union, to contemporary Russia, and is probably the most difficult to change not only because of structures but also because of the attitudes of those in power.

As Sparks has noted, the situation that has emerged after the end of Communism suggests a new position, in which the relationship between politics and economics is one neither of identity nor of complete separation, but of interpenetration (2000b, 42–43). He further observes that the alignment of different sections of capital with various political forces can be seen at its extreme in what I. Zassoursky calls "political" capital in contemporary Russia. It can be understood as an effort by the political element to gain access to sources of power, and by the economic element to secure a position of advantage in the competitive struggle. The allegations that Gusinsky took part in the theft of state funds in a deal to sell state enterprise support this analysis—the interpenetration of politics and economics offers the government a way to interfere through the latter when it is increasingly difficult to do it through politics.

In this situation, the question of who controls the national media system becomes extremely important. Full control, as it existed in the former Soviet Union, is impossible not only for political reasons but because of the variety of media and communications available to individual citizens. Globalization has brought individual access to media and communications that are not completely controlled by national media systems. In that sense, Russians live in an entirely new period, although all people do not have equal access to these means of communications. Nevertheless, national media systems exist and indigenize global elements, particularly on television. National media systems are less powerful, but they have not withered away.

THE IMPACT OF EVIDENCE FROM POST-COMMUNIST RUSSIA ON GLOBALIZATION THEORIES

The case of post-Communist Russia contributes to our understanding of globalization in several ways. First, any theorization on globalization should include non-Western countries. Otherwise, we mainly talk about Westernization instead of globalization. Second, any globalization theories should include media and communications, because as the Russian case study shows, their importance is crucial not only in cultural globalization, but also as a key element in every globalization process, be it political, economic, or cultural. Media and communications glue together different globalization processes, an argument that becomes more concrete when we look at different theoretical issues raised by globalization theorists.

In the Russian case, as elsewhere in Central and Eastern Europe, the process of globalization takes place simultaneously with the process of nationalization. A new nationhood is being constructed in circumstances where the media is being exposed to globalization after decades of isolation. This process is called natio-globalization, the restructuring of the global and the national, and the media play a key role in this process. Media and communications are reforming nation-states, and a new global society is emerging as a consequence of shared technology and economy. Giddens (1999) remarks that global society theory is driven by communications technology. In fact, most globalization theorists have mainly been interested in this emerging global society, but they fail to acknowledge that national society theory is also changed and driven by communication technology. It is not only that globalization takes certain powers away from nations, but that globalization also fundamentally changes them. The global has come to stay in the national, and what we witness today is the new formation of the global and the national. It is pointless to argue whether a system is national or global, because every national media system has been globalized in one way or another, whether in technology, ownership, structure, or content.

It is not a question of either globalization *or* nation-states, but a question of the global becoming present in the national—national media structures encountering globalization. When this takes place, when the global meets the national, both change. Globalization becomes nationalized, because the national not only absorbs or assimilates, but even resists globalization. The result is never the same, but is always a transformed form of globalization—nationalized globalization. And media and communications play a key role in this process.

It is also important to note the role of the state in this process. As Billig has observed, the "nation" carries two interrelated meanings: the nation as the nation-state and the nation as the people living within the state (1995, 24). In post-Communist Russia, in both meanings, it is possible to see resistance to globalization. But the primary force against globalization, both in the Soviet era and in post-Communist Russia, is the state. The "nation" and the state might not go hand in hand in the way they used to, but together they are a powerful barrier against globalization.

THE IMPACT OF EVIDENCE FROM POST-COMMUNIST RUSSIA ON MEDIA AND COMMUNICATIONS THEORIES

Like globalization theories, media imperialism theories have taken the national as the antithesis of the global, ignoring the fact that national media systems are not homogenous entities, but are composed of different elements not necessarily in harmony with each other. Such theories have repeatedly expressed concern about the future of the national media systems, and even about national cultures. In this book, choosing four different case studies to represent the different sections of Russian media was a deliberate attempt to pay attention not only to the similarities, but also to the differences inside a single media and communications system.

These differences have wider consequences for our understanding of globalization. Whatever the process of globalization is—political, economic, or cultural—the media increasingly have a part in it. Because of media and globalization, no nation-state can opt out of globalization. Rather, they become in one way or another a part of the global network society, either through media economy, structures, contents, technology, policy, or consumption—all of which now exceed national boundaries. However, in contrast to what is argued in media imperialism theory, national media systems are not losing their power. They still act as intermediaries, because what takes place in the economy does not necessarily take place simultaneously, let us say, in policy. National media systems get globalized without policy, but they remain partly national, even if there is no governmental policy, simply because of existing structures and long-lasting practices. Only very rarely, as was the case in the October Revolution, can the different parts of the national media system be changed simultaneously and completely. Nowadays, because of the availability of new technology, it has become almost impossible to take control over the whole media and communications system. The different parts are on the move unevenly, sometimes simply changing very slowly and, when they do, changes always take place in the interaction between the old and the new. As Appadurai says about different cultural flows, there are also junctures and disjunctures in them in the same way as there are between the old and the new media—between their economy, structures, contents, technology, policy, and consumption (1990). What we need to accept is that that the era of purely national media systems (if it ever existed) and audiences is over, and that there are increasingly global elements in them. Likewise, there is no pure global media (if there ever was), but they must operate in national contexts.

This is why the fashionable dichotomy of the global and the local is partially misleading. Increasingly, media scholars use the term "local" when they actually speak of the national. The Russian case, and I believe other cases as well (see, for example, Curran and Park 2000), indicates that the national is not withering away. It is important that the "national" is not replaced in actual research with the "local." The national is still very much alive, but transformed into a combination of the global and the national.

Neither does the experience of globalization take place in a vacuum. Global experiences, mainly provided by the national mass media, which transform them into a national product (dubbing, buying foreign formats, making advertisements to meet the taste of the local audience), are finally localized by consumption. There is an agreement that, due to media, most people can now lead dual lives—they can have simultaneous access to "here" and "there." In this sense, their life is more globalized in their own local communities than it has ever been. But, their experience is not necessarily universal. Increased globalization can result in increased nationalism when there is too much globalization. Increased nationalism can result in increased globalization when there is no access beyond the national. There are no simple answers. The purely national has been broken, and it is not being replaced by the purely global, but by a combination of both. What is important is that there is no way of going back to the era of the pure national that has been changed profoundly. Globalization is here to stay, but it takes multiple forms in different countries. By studying countries like Russia we understand how diverse its consequences are.

References

Albrow, Martin. 1996. *The Global Age: State and Society Beyond Modernity*. Cambridge: Polity Press.

Anderson, Benedict. 1983. *Imagined Communities: Reflections on the Origin and Spread of Nationalism*. London: Verso.

Androunas, Elena. 1993. *Soviet Media in Transition: Structural and Economic Alternatives*. Westport, Conn.: Praeger.

Appadurai, Arjun. 1990. "Disjuncture and Difference in the Global Cultural Economy." *Public Culture* 2 (3): 1–23.

———. 1996. *Modernity at Large: Cultural Dimensions of Globalization*. Minneapolis: University of Minneapolis Press.

Avdeenko, Sergei, and Dmitrii Pinsker. 1999. "Khoziaeva gosudarstvennykh 'Novostei' (The Proprietors of the State-owned Novosti)." *Itogi* 11: 16–18.

"A Bad Time to Be an Ostrich." 1998. *The Economist*, 19 December.

Baldwin, Kate. 1995. "Montezuma's Revenge: Reading *Los Ricos También Lloran* in Russia." In *To Be Continued. . . Soap Operas Around the World*, edited by Robert C. Allen, 285–300. London: Routledge.

Barker, Chris. 1997. *Global Television: An Introduction*. Oxford: Blackwell.

Bauman, Zygmund. 1992. *Intimations of Postmodernity*. London: Routledge.

Beck, Ulrich. 2000. *What is Globalization?* Cambridge: Polity Press.

"Better Data, Global Expertise Benefit Advertising." 1995. *Economist Intelligence Unit* 13/7. Reuters Business Briefing.

Billig, Michael. 1995. *Banal Nationalism*. London: Sage.

Borenstein, Eliot. 1999. "Public Offerings: MMM and the Marketing of

Melodrama." In *Consuming Russia: Popular Culture, Sex, and Society since Gorbachev*, edited by Adele Marie Barker, 49–75. Durham, N.C.: Duke University Press.

Boretskii, Rudolph A. 1998. *V bermudskom treugol'nike TV* (In the Bermuda Triangle of Television). Moscow: Isdatel'stvo Ikar.

Boyd, Douglas A. 1989. "The Videocassette Recorder in the USSR and Soviet Block." In *The VCR Age: Home Video and Mass Communication*, edited by Mark R. Levy, 252–70. Newbury Park: Sage.

Boyd-Barrett, Oliver. 1977. "Media Imperialism: Towards an International Framework for the Analysis of Media Systems." In *Mass Media and Society*, edited by James Curran and Michael Gurevitch, 116–35. London: Edward Arnold.

———. 1998. "Media Imperialism Reformulated." In *Electronic Empires: Global Media and Local Resistance*, edited by Daya Kishan Thussu, 157–76. London: Edward Arnold.

———. 2000. "Constructing the Global, Constructing the Local: News Agencies Re-Present the World." In *The Global Dynamics of News: Studies in International News Coverage and News Agenda*, edited by Abbas Malek and Anandam P. Kavoori, 299–322. Stamford, Conn.: Ablex.

Boyd-Barrett, Oliver, and Terhi Rantanen, eds. 1998. *The Globalization of News*. London: Sage.

———. 1998. "The Globalization of News." In *The Globalization of News*, edited by Oliver Boyd-Barrett and Terhi Rantanen, 1–14. London: Sage.

———. 2000. "European National News Agencies: The End of an Era or a New Beginning." *Journalism: Theory, Practice and Criticism* 1(1):86–105.

Boym, Svetlana. 1994. *Common Places: Mythologies of Everyday Life in Russia*. Cambridge: Harvard University Press.

Bryan, Cathy, Roza Tsagarousianou, and Damian Tambini. 1998. "Electronic Democracy and the Civic Networking Movement in Context." In *Cyberdemocracy: Technology, Cities and Civic Networks*, edited by Roza Tsagarousianou, Damian Tambini, and Cathy Bryan, 1–17. London: Routledge.

Carnoy, Martin, Manuel Castells, Stephen S. Cohen, and Fernando Henrique Cardoso. 1993. *The New Global Economy in the Information Age: Reflections on Our Changing World*. University Park: The Pennsylvania State University Press.

Castells, Manuel. 1996. *The Rise of the Network Society*. Oxford: Blackwell.

———. 1997. *The Power of Identity*. Oxford: Blackwell.

———. 1998. *The Information Age: Economy, Society, and Culture*. Vol. 3. Oxford: Blackwell.

Collins, Richard. 1990. *Television: Policy and Culture*. London: Unwin Hyman.

——. 1998. *From Satellite to Single Market: New Communication Technology and European Public Service Television*. London: Routledge.

"Communists Call for State 'Media Propaganda Centre.'" 1998. *Post-Soviet Media Law & Policy Newsletter*, no. 50, 1 November, 10–11.

Condee, Nancy, and Vladimir Padunov. 1995. "The ABC of Russian Consumer Culture: Readings, Ratings and Real Estate." In *Soviet Hieroglyphics: Visual Culture in Late Twentieth Century Russia*, edited by Nancy Condee, 130–69. Bloomington: Indiana University Press.

Curran, James, and Myung-Jin Park. 2000. "Beyond Globalization Theory." In *De-Westernizing Media Studies*, edited by James Curran and Myung-Jin Park, 3–18. London: Routledge.

Davies, Gareth, Steve Carter, Stuart McIntosh, and Dan Stefanescu. 1996. "Technology and Policy Options for the Telecommunications Sector: The Situation in Central and Eastern Europe and the Former Soviet Union." *Telecommunications Policy* 20 (2): 101–23.

Denisov, L. 1996. "Struggles on the Steppes." *Telecom International* (September): 10–14.

"Diversity and Disarray." 1997. *Public Network Europe Yearbook*: 88–91.

Dizard, Wilson P., and Blake S. Swensrud. 1987. *Gorbachev's Information Revolution: Controlling Glasnost in a New Electronic Era*. Significant Issues Series, vol. 4, no. 8. Boulder, Colo.: Westview Press.

Downing, J. D. H. 1989a. "International Communications and the Second World: Developments in Communication Strategies." *European Journal of Communication* 4 (1): 117–37.

——. 1989b. "Computers for Political Change: Peacenet and Public Data Access." *Journal of Communication* 39 (3): 154–79.

Downing, John. 1996. *Internationalizing Media Theory: Transition, Power, Culture*. London: Sage.

Dutkina, Galina. 1996. *Moscow Days: Life and Hard Times in the New Russia*. New York: Kodansha America.

Dziadul, Chris. 1998. *Television in Central and Eastern Europe*. London: Financial Times.

Ekecrantz, Jan. 1998. "Globalization/Textualization." Paper presented at the International Association for Media and Communication Research Conference in Glasgow.

Ellis, Frank. 1998. "The Media as Social Engineer." In *Russian Cultural Studies: An Introduction*, edited by Catriona Kelly and David Shepherd, 192–222. Oxford: Oxford University Press.

——. 1999. *From Glasnost to the Internet: Russia's New Infosphere*. London: Macmillan Press.

Evstafiev, V. 2000. Telephone interview, March.

Evtiushkin, A. V. 1998. "Zhurnalistika v Internete: Osobennosti stanovleniia SMI novogo tipa" (Journalism in the Internet: Characteristics of the development of the new type mass media). In *Zhurnalistika v perehkodnyi period: problemy i perspektivy. Materialy mezhdunarodnoi nauchnoi konferentsii* (Journalism in the Transition Period: Problems and Perspectives. Materials of the International Scientific Conference), 81–85. Moscow: Department of Journalism at Moscow State University.

Featherstone, Mike. 1995. *Undoing Culture: Globalization, Postmodernism and Identity.* London: Sage.

Featherstone, Mike, and Scott Lash. 1995. "Globalization, Modernity and the Spatialization of Social Theory: An Introduction." In *Global Modernities*, edited by Mike Featherstone and Scott Lash, 1–24. London: Sage.

Feher, Ferenc, Agnes Heller, and Györky Markus. 1983. *Dictatorship over Needs: An Analysis of Soviet Societies.* Oxford: Basil Blackwell.

Feldbrugge, F. J. M. 1975. *Samizdat and Political Dissent in the Soviet Union.* Leyden: A. W. Sijthoff.

Feofanov, Oleg. 2000. *Reklama: Novye tekhnologii v Rossi* (Advertising: New technology in Russia). St. Petersburg: Peter.

Fiks, Sergei. 1998. Interview by author. Moscow, 18 November.

Ganley, Gladys. 1992. *The Exploding Political Power of Personal Media.* Norwood, N.J.: Ablex.

———. 1996. *Unglued Empire: The Soviet Experience with Communications Technologies.* Norwood, N.J.: Ablex.

Gellner, Ernest. 1983. *Nations and Nationalism.* Oxford: Blackwell.

Giddens, Anthony. 1990. *The Consequences of Modernity.* Cambridge: Polity Press.

———. 1991. *Modernity and Self-Identity: Self and Society in the Late Modern Age.* Cambridge: Polity Press.

———. 1999. "Runaway World: The Reith Lectures Revisited—Globalization" (10 November 1999), www.lse.ac.uk/Depts/Media/GlobalMedia/globalisation.html.

Globalization of the Mass Media. 1993. Department of Commerce, National Telecommunications and Information Administration. Washington: Government Printing Office.

Goban-Klas, Tomasz. 1994. *The Orchestration of the Media: The Politics of Mass Communications in Communist Poland and the Aftermath.* Boulder, Colo.: Westview Press.

Golding, Peter, and Philip Harris (eds). 1997. *Beyond Cultural Imperialism: Globalization, Communication, and the New International Order.* London: Sage.

Goodman, Seymour E. 1988. "Information Societies." In *The Future Infor-*

mation Revolution in the USSR, edited by Richard F. Staar, 11–18. New York: Crane Russak & Company.

Gourko, Elena. 1993. "Democratization and Media in Deconstructive Perspective." In *Media in Transition*, edited by Oleg Manaev and Yurii Pryluk, 46–64. Kiev: Avris.

Graffy, Julian. 1998 "Cinema." In *Russian Cultural Studies: An Introduction*, edited by Catriona Kelly and David Shepherd, 165–91. Oxford: Oxford University Press.

Graham, Loren R. 1998. *What Have We Learned About Science and Technology from the Russian Experience?* Stanford, Calif.: Stanford University Press.

Gray, John. 1998. *False Dawn: The Delusions of Global Capitalism*. London: Granta Books.

Gronow, Jukka. 1997. *The Sociology of Taste*. London: Routledge.

Gutterman, Steven. 1994. "Russians Quick to Embrace Ads as Comrades." *Advertising Age*, no. 6: 19. Reuters Business Briefing.

Hamelink, Cees. 1983. *Cultural Autonomy in Global Communications*. New York: Longman.

Hanson, Philip. 1974. *Advertising and Socialism*. London: Macmillan.

Harvey, David. 1989. *The Condition of Modernity*. Oxford: Blackwell.

———. 1993. "From Space to Place and Back again: Reflections on the Condition of Postmodernity." In *Mapping the Futures: Local Culture, Global Change*, edited by Jon Bird et al., 3–29. London: Routledge.

Helin, Antti. 1999. "Miten kävi neukuilta rock 'n' roll?" *Yliopisto: Acta Universitatis Helsingiensis*, no 9: 33–35.

Herman, Edward, and Robert W. McChesney. 1997. *The Global Media: The New Missionaries of Global Capitalism*. London: Cassell.

Hirst, Paul, and Graham Thompson. 1996. *Globalization in Question*. Cambridge: Polity Press.

Hopkins, Mark W. 1970. *Mass Media in the Soviet Union*. New York: Pegasus.

Hoskins, Colin, Stuart McFadyen, and Adam Finn. 1997. *Global Television and Film: An Introduction to the Economics of Business*. Oxford: Clarendon Press.

Iampol'skaia, R. M., and A. S. Serkova. 1998. "Izdatel'skii kontsern 'Burda'—Rossiiskomu chitateliu" (Publishing Concern 'Burda' —To the Russian Reader). In *Zhurnalistika v perekhodyi period: problemy i perspektivy.* "Mezhdunarodnoi nauchnoi konferentsii" (Journalism in the Transition Period: Problems and Perspectives. Materials of the International Scientific Conference): 118–25. Moscow: Department of Journalism, Moscow State University.

Ignatenko, Vitaly. 1999. Interview by author. Moscow, 28 June.

Jack, Andrew, and Arkady Ostrovsky. 2000. "Russian Summons Steps up Pressure on Two Oligarchs." *Financial Times,* 2 November.

Jakubowicz, Karol. 1997. "The Empire Strikes East." *The Bulletin of the European Institute for the Media* 14(1): 4–5.

———. 1998. "Improving on the West—the Native Way: Poland." In *The Development of the Audiovisual Landscape in Central Europe since 1989,* 253–84. Luton: ULP/John Libbey Media.

Kelly, Catriona. 1998. "Creating a Consumer." In *Russian Cultural Studies: An introduction,* edited by Catriona Kelly and David Shepherd, 223–43. Oxford: Oxford University Press.

Kelly, Catriona, David Shepherd, and Stephen White. 1998. "Toward Post-Soviet Pluralism." In *Russian Cultural Studies An Introduction,* edited by Catriona Kelly and David Shepherd, 387–400. Oxford: Oxford University Press.

Kivikuru, Ullamaija. 1988. "From Import to Modelling: Finland—An Example of Old Periphery Dependency." *European Journal of Communication* 3 (1): 9–34.

Kolar-Panov, Dona. 1997. *Video, War, and the Diasporic Imagination.* London: Routledge.

Kolesnik, Svetlana. 1991. "Advertising and Cultural Politics." *Journal of Communication* 41 (2): 46–54.

———. 1997. "Television and Politics: The ORT Crisis." *Post-Soviet Media Law & Policy Newsletter* no. 37, 13 June, 9–12.

Komissar, Mikhail. 1992. Interview by author. Moscow, 23 July.

Kon, Igor S. 1996. "Moral Culture." In *Russian Culture at the Crossroads: Paradoxes of Post-Communist Consciousness,* edited by Dmitri N. Shalin, 185–208. Boulder, Colo.: Westview Press.

Laclau, Ernesto. 1990. *New Reflections on the Revolution of Our Time.* London: Verso.

Larrain, Jorge. 1994. *Ideology and Cultural Identity: Modernity and the Third World Presence.* Cambridge: Polity Press.

Larsen, Susan. 1999. "In Search of an Audience: The New Russian Cinema of Reconciliation." In *Consuming Russia: Popular Culture, Sex, and Society since Gorbachev,* edited by Adele Marie Barker, 192–216. Durham, N.C.: Duke University Press.

"Lazutkin Assesses State of Russian TV." 1996. In *Post-Soviet Media Law & Policy Newsletter,* no. 33–34, 12–14.

Lengyel, Emöke. 1998. "The Art of Careful Power Balancing: Hungary." In *The Development of the Audiovisual Landscape in Central Europe since 1989,* 139–202. Luton: ULP/John Libbey Media.

Livingstone, Sonia. 1999. "New Media, New Audiences." *New Media and Society* 1 (1): 59–66.

Loshchak, V. 1997. "Gromootvod rossiiskoi pressy (The Lightning Conductor of the Russian Press)." *Moskovskie novosti* (January): 12–19.

Loukina, Marina. 2000. "Factors of E-media developments: An experience of media mapping RUNET." Paper presented at the International Association for Media and Communication Research Conference, Singapore, 17–20 July.

Lull, James. 1995. *Media, Communication, Culture: A Global Approach.* Cambridge: Polity Press.

Lutz, Michel P. and Jaromir Jankowski. 1998. "Radio and Television Systems in Russia." In *Radio and Television Systems in Central and Eastern Europe*, edited by Hans Bredow, 62–81. Strasbourg: European Audiovisual Observatory.

Manaev, Oleg. 1991. "The Influence of Western Radio on the Democratization of Soviet Youth." *Journal of Communication* 41 (2): 72–91.

———. 1993. "The Alternative Press in a Transnational Society." In *Alternative Media: Linking Global and Local*. Reports and Papers on Mass Communication, no. 107. Edited by Peter Lewis. Paris: UNESCO.

Mårtenson, Gunnar. 1998. Finnet International Services via Russian Counterparts. Memo, 29 May.

McDaniel, Tim. 1996. *The Agony of the Russian Idea*. Princeton: Princeton University Press.

McHenry, William K. 1988. "Computer Networks and the Soviet-style Information Society." In *The Future Information Revolution in the USSR*, edited by Richard F. Staar, 85–114. New York: Crane Russak & Company.

McKay, Betsy. 1998. "Moscow Diary. Worries to Worse: Revisiting a Family in Russia Seven Years On." *The Wall Street Journal Europe*, 29 September.

McKay, Betsy, and Steven Gutterman. 1994. "For Ads, Russian Revolution Lives." *Advertising Age*, no. 3: 40.

McNair, Brian. 1991. *Glasnost, Perestroika, and the Soviet Media*. London: Routledge.

———. 2000. "Power, Profit, Corruption, and Lies: The Russian Media in the 1990s." In *De-Westernizing Media Studies*, edited by James Curran and Myung-Jin Park, 79–94. London: Routledge.

Meier, Werner A., and Josef Trappel. 1998. "Media Concentration and the Public Interest." In *Media Policy: Convergence, Concentration, and Commerce*, edited by Denis McQuail and Karen Siune, 38–59. London: Sage.

Meliukhin, I. S. 1997. *Informatsionnye tekhnologii i biznes* (Information Technologies and Business). Moscow: Garant-Park.

Melvin, Neil. 1995. *Russians Beyond Russia: The Politics of National Identity*. The Royal Institute of International Affairs. Chatham House papers. London: Pinter.

Mickiewitcz, Ellen. 1988. *Split Signals: Television and Politics in the Soviet Union.* New York: Oxford University Press.

———. 1997. *Changing Channels: Television and the Struggle for Power in Russia.* New York: Oxford University Press.

———. 1999. *Changing Channels: Television and the Struggle for Power in Russia.* Revised and expanded edition. Durham, N.C.: Duke University Press.

Mironenko, N. N., and E. N. Mironenko. 1998. "Independent Media na informatsionom rynke Rossii" (Independent Media in the Russian Informational Market). *Zhurnalistika v perekhodnyi period: problemy i perspektivy. Materialy mezhdunarodnoy nauchnoi konferentsii* (Journalism in the Transition Period: Problems and Perspectives. Materials of the International Scientific Conference). Moscow: Department of Journalism, Moscow State University.

Mochenov, Andrei. 1998. "Monstry' rynka informatsii (The Monsters of the Information Market)." *Finansovaia Rossiia* 3 (January): 1, 6.

Morley, David, and Kevin Robins. 1995. *Spaces of Identity: Global Media, Electronic Landscapes and Cultural Boundaries.* London: Routledge.

Murdoch, Graham. 1993. "Communications and the Constitutions of Modernity." *Media, Culture, and Society* 15 (4): 573–98.

Nelson, Michael. 1998. *War of the Black Heavens: The Battles of Western Broadcasting in the Cold War.* Syracuse, N.Y.: Syracuse University Press.

Neumann, Iber B. 1996. *Russia and the Idea of Europe: A Study in Identity and International Relations.* London: Routledge.

Noam, Eli. 1991. *Television in Europe.* Oxford: Oxford University Press.

Nordenstreng, Kaarle, and Osmo A. Wiio. 1986. *Suomen viestintäjärjestelmä* (Finland's Communications System). Tampere: Weilin + Göös.

———. 1994. *Joukkoviestintä Suomessa* (Mass Communication in Finland). Porvoo: Weilin + Göös.

Nordenstreng, Kaarle, and Tapio Varis. 1974. "Television Traffic—A One Way Street? A Survey and Analysis of the International Flow of Television Programme Material." Reports and Papers on Mass Communication, no. 40. Paris: UNESCO.

Nurpeissov, Timur. 1998a. "A Former Soviet's View of California, the United States." *The Business Journal*, 8 June.

———. 1998b. "Lessons Kazakhstan Learned from Its Venture into Capitalism." *The Business Journal*, 25 May.

———. 2000. Interview by author, 28 April.

"O sredstvakh massovoi informatsii." 1996. In *Zakonodatel'stvo Rossiiskoi Federatsii o sredstvakh massovoi informatsii* (Mass Media Legislation in the Russian Federation), 7–34. Moscow: Gardarika.

Ob informatsionnom telegrafnom agentstve Rossii (ITAR). 1993. Ukaz prezidenta (Presidential decree concerning ITAR). Moscow, 22 December no. 2257.

Ohmae, Kenichi. 1995. *The End of the Nation State: The Rise of Regional Economies*. London: Harper Collins Publishers.

Olson, Olga. 1999. Interview by author. Moscow, 18 November.

Orlova, Irina. 1991. "Notes from the Underground: The Emergence of Rock Music." *Journal of Communication* 41 (1): 66–71.

Paasilinna, Reino. 1995. *Glasnost and Soviet Television: A Study of the Soviet Mass Media and Its Role in Society From 1985–1991*. Finnish Broadcasting Company, Research Report 5.

Palmer, Michael. 1998. "What Makes News." In *The Globalization of News*, edited by Oliver Boyd-Barret and Terhi Rantanen, 125–36. London: Sage.

Palmer, Michael, Oliver Boyd-Barrett, and Terhi Rantanen. 1998. "Global Financial News." In *The Globalization of News*, edited by Oliver Boyd-Barrett and Terhi Rantanen, 61–78. London: Sage.

"Paper Views Effects on ORT of Advertising Crisis." 1998. *Post-Soviet Media Law & Policy Newsletter*, no. 50, 1 November, 6.

Pearson, Raymond. 1998. *The Rise and Fall of the Soviet Empire*. Houndmills, England: Macmillan Press.

Philips, Alan. 1995. "Russians Refuse to Fall for the West's Hard Sell." *Sunday Telegraph*, 23 March.

Pieterse, Jan Nederveen. 1995. "Globalization as Hybridization." In *Global Modernities*, edited by Mike Featherstone, Scott Lash, and Roland Robertson, 45–68. London: Sage.

Pishikova, E. 1995. "General slovarnogo zapasa (General of the Lexical Reserve)." *Obschaia gazeta*, 8–14 June.

Poroikov, Iurii. 1995. "Budem li my rabami Reiter (Shall We Become Reuters' Slaves?)." *Obschaia gazeta*, 15–31 May.

Price, Monroe E. 1995. *Television, the Public Sphere, and National Identity*. Oxford: Clarendon Press.

Rantanen, Terhi. 1980. "Kaksi kanavaa—kaksi maailmaa: The *New York Times* in ja *Pravdan* ulkomaanaineisto" (Two channels—two worlds: Foreign news in the *New York Times* and *Pravda*). Unpublished master's thesis, Department of Communication, Helsinki University.

———. 1990. *Foreign News in Imperial Russia: The Relationship between Russian and International News Agencies, 1856–1914*. Helsinki: Suomalainen Tiedeakatemia.

———. 1994. *Howard Interviews Stalin: How the AP, UP, and TASS Smashed the International News Cartel*. Roy W. Howard Monographs in Journalism and Mass Communication Research, no 3. Bloomington: Indiana University, School of Journalism.

———. 1998. "From Communism to Capitalism." In *The Globalization of News*, edited by Oliver Boyd-Barrett and Terhi Rantanen, 125–36. London: Sage.

Rantanen, Terhi, and Elena Vartanova. 1993. *From State Monopoly to Competition: The Changing Landscape of News Agencies in Russia.* University of Helsinki, Department of Communication, Publications 1C/1.

———. 1995. "News Agencies in Post-Communist Russia: From State Monopoly to State Dominance." *European Journal of Communication* 10 (2): 207–20.

———. 1997. "News Agencies in Post-Communist Russia: From State Monopoly to the 'Big Three.'" Unpublished manuscript.

Raskine, Andrei. 2000. "The Russian Presidential Election Campaigns and the National Television, 1991–2000." Paper presented at the 22d General Assembly and Scientific Conference in Singapore, July 17–20.

Regli, Brian J. W. 1997. *Wireless: Strategically Liberalizing the Telecommunications Market.* Mahwah, N.J.: Lawrence Erlbaum Associates.

"RIA Agency Becomes Subsidiary of VGTRK." 1998. *Post-Soviet Media Law & Policy Newsletter,* no. 47, 15 June, 7–8.

Rice, Ronald. 1999. "Artifacts and Paradoxes in New Media." *New Media and Society* 1 (1): 23–32.

Richter, Andrei G. 2000. "Media Regulation in Russia." Paper presented at the International Association for Media and Communication Conference in Singapore, 17–20 July.

Riordan, James, Christopher Williams, and Igor Ilynsky. 1995. *Young People in Post-Communist Russia and Eastern Europe.* Aldershot, England: Dartmouth.

Robertson, Roland. 1990. "Mapping the Global Condition: Globalization as the Central Concept." In *Theory, Culture, and Society,* 15–30. London: Sage.

———. 1995. "Glocalization: Time-Space and Homogeneity-Heterogeneity." In *Global Modernities,* edited by Mike Featherstone, Scott Lash, and Roland Robertson, 25–44. London: Sage.

Rohde, Carl C., and Carsten R. C. Pellikaan. 1995. "Advertising and the Legitimacy Crisis of Eastern Europe." In *Communication in Eastern Europe: The Role of History, Culture and Media in Contemporary Conflicts,* edited by Fred L. Casmir, 133–63. Mahwah, N.J.: Lawrence Erlbaum Associates Publishers.

Rose, Richard. 1996. *New Russian Barometer V: Between Two Elections.* Studies in Public Policy, no. 260. Glasgow: Centre for the Study of Public Policy, University of Strathclyde.

Ryback, Timothy W. 1990. *Rock Around the Block: A History of Rock Music in Eastern Europe and the Soviet Union.* New York: Oxford University Press.

Scannell, Paddy. 1989. "Public Service Broadcasting and Modern Life." *Media, Culture, and Society* 11 (1): 135–66.

Shane, Scott. 1994. *Dismantling Utopia: How Information Ended the Soviet Union*. Chicago: I. R. Dee.

Shlapentokh, Vladimir. 1989. *Public and Private Life of the Soviet People: Changing Values in Post-Stalin Russia*. New York: Oxford University Press.

Sinclair, John, Elizabeth Jacka, and Stuart Cunningham. 1996. "Peripheral Vision." In *New Patterns in Global Television: Peripheral Vision*, edited by John Sinclair, Elizabeth Jacka, and Stuart Cunningham, 1–31. Oxford: Oxford University Press.

Sklair, Leslie. 1995. *Sociology of the Global System*. 2d ed. London: Prentice Hall.

Sosnovsky, Anatolii. 1998. Interview by author. Moscow, 16 November.

Soviet Mass Media: Aims and Organization, Past and Present. 1979. Moscow: Novosti Press Agency Publishing House.

Sparks, Colin. 1995. "Introduction to Emerging Media Systems of Postcommunism." *Public* 2 (3): 7–17.

———. 1998. "Is There a Global Public Sphere?" In *Electronic Empires: Global Media and Local Resistance*, edited by Daya Kishan Thussu. London: Edward Arnold.

———. 2000a. "The Global, the Local and the Public Sphere." In *The New Communications Landscape: Demystifying Media Globalization*, edited by Georgette Wang, Jan Servaes, and Aneera Goonasekera, 74–95. London: Routledge.

———. 2000b. "Media Theory after the Fall of European Communism: Why the Old Models from East and West Won't Do Any More." In *De-Westernizing Media Studies*, edited by James Curran and Myung-Jin Park, 35–39. London: Routledge.

Sparks, Colin, and Anna Reading. 1998. *Communism, Capitalism and the Mass Media*. London: Sage.

Splichal, Slavko. 1994. *Media Beyond Socialism: Theory and Practice in East-Central Europe*. Boulder, Colo.: Westview Press.

Sreberny-Mohammadi, Annabelle. 1996. "The Global and the Local in International Communications." In *Mass Media and Society*, edited by James Curran and Michael Gurevitch, 177–203. London: Edward Arnold.

Sreberny-Mohammadi, Annabelle, and Ali Mohammadi. 1994. *Small Media, Big Revolution: Communication, Culture and the Iranian Revolution*. Minneapolis: University of Minnesota Press.

Sreberny-Mohammadi, Annabelle, with Kaarle Nordenstreng, Robert Stevenson, and Frank Ugboajah. 1985. "Foreign News in the Media: International Reporting in Twenty-Nine Countries." Final report of the "Foreign Images" study undertaken for UNESCO by the International Association for Media and Communication Research. Reports and Papers on Mass Communication, no. 93. Paris: UNESCO.

Sredstva massovoi informatsii Rossii 1997 god. Analiz. Tendentsii. Prognoz (Russian Mass Media in 1997. Analysis. Tendencies. Prognos). 1998. Soiuz zhurnalistov Rossii. Moscow: Infotsentr.

"Staff Cuts at RIA Novosti." 1998. *Post-Soviet Media Law and Policy Newsletter* no. 50, 1 November, 10–11.

Starr, S. Frederick. 1984. "Technology and Freedom in the Soviet Union." *Technology Review* (May/June): 38–47.

Thomas, John R. 1998. "Soviet Scientific-Technical Performance: A Framework for the USSR's Information Revolution." In *The Future Information Revolution in the USSR*, edited by Richard F. Staar, 155–74. New York: Crane Russak.

Thompson, John B. 1995. *The Media and Modernity: A Social Theory of the Media.* Cambridge: Polity Press.

Thornhill, John. 1998a. "Sweet Taste of Success." *Financial Times*, 4 January.

———. 1998b. "The Fallen Colossus." *Financial Times*, 31 December.

Thussu, Daya Kishan, ed. 1998. *Electronic Empires: Global Media and Local Resistance.* London: Edward Arnold.

Tomlinson, John. 1991. *Cultural Imperialism: A Critical Introduction.* Baltimore: Johns Hopkins University Press.

———. 1994. "A Phenomenology of Globalization? Giddens on Global Modernity." *European Journal of Communication* 9 (2): 149–72.

———. 1997. "Cultural Globalization and Cultural Imperialism." In *International Communication and Globalization*, edited by Ali Mohammed, 170–90. London: Sage.

———. 1999. *Globalization and Culture.* Cambridge: Polity Press.

Törmänen, Kirsi. 1997. "Gzha Varota eli Ms. Gate. Portinvartijat Venäjän joukkoviestinnässä" (Gzha Varota or Ms. Gate: Gate-keepers in the Russian Mass Media). Unpublished Master's thesis. Department of Communication, Helsinki University.

Trappel, Joseph, and David Mahon. 1998. "Television in the Enlarged European Audiovisual Area —A Community Perspective." In *The Development of the Audiovisual Landscape in Central Europe since 1989*, 15–26. Luton: ULP/John Libbey Media.

Troitsky, Artemy. 1987. *Back in the USSR: The True Story of Rock in Russia.* London: Omnibus.

Tunstall, Jeremy, and David Machin. 1999. *The Anglo-American Media Connection.* Oxford: Oxford University Press.

Ukaz Prezidenta Rossiiskoi Federatsii of informatsionnom telegrafnom agentstve Rossii (ITAR). 1992. (Presidential decree concerning ITAR). Moscow, 22 January.

Varis, Tapio. 1984. "The International Flow of Television Programmes." *Journal of Communication* 34 (1): 143–52.

Vartanova, Elena. 1991. *The Soviet Media in 1991*. Department of Communication. University of Helsinki Publications. Series 1C/1/92.

———. 1997. "The Russian Financial Elite as Media Moguls." *Post-Soviet Media Law & Policy Newsletter*, no. 35, 27 February, 18–23.

———. 1998a. "National Infrastructure for the New Media in Russia." In *Changing Media and Communications: Concepts, Technologies and Ethic in Global and National Perspectives*, edited by Yassen N. Zassoursky and Elena Vartanova, 174–88. Moscow: Faculty of Journalism/Publisher IKAR.

———. 1998b. "Natsional'naia infrastruktura novykh media v Rossii" (National Infrastructure of the New Media in Russia). In *Zhurnalistika v perehkodnyi period: problemy i perspektivy. Materialy mezhdunarodnoi nauchnoi konferentsii* (Journalism in the Transition Period: Problems and Perspectives. Materials of the International Scientific Conference). Moscow: Department of Journalism, Moscow State University.

———. 2000. "Media in Post-Communist Russia: Shifts in Structures and Access to Contents." Paper presented at the 22d General Assembly and Scientific Conference in Singapore, July 17–20.

Vladimirnovna, A. L. 1998. Interview by author, July.

Volin, Aleksei K. 1999. Interview by author. Moscow, 29 June.

Warde, Alen. 1994. "Consumption, Identity-Formation and Uncertainty." *Sociology* 28 (4): 877–98.

Waters, Malcolm. 1995. *Globalization*. London: Routledge.

Woodward, Kathryn. 1997. "Concepts of Identity and Difference." In *Identity and Difference*, edited by Kathryn Woodward, 8–66. London: Sage.

World Communication Report. 1989. Paris: UNESCO.

World Telecommunication Development Report. 1998. Geneve: International Telecommunication Union.

Wyman, Matthew. 1997. *Public Opinion in Post-Communist Russia*. Houndmills, England: Macmillan Press.

"Yeltsin Approves Ostankino 'Privatization': Twelve Companies to Share Ownership with State." 1994. *Post-Communist Media Law & Policy Newsletter*, 10 December, 1.

Yrjämä-Rantinoja, Tellervo. 1992. "Lännen dollarit uhkaavat Venäjän tiedonvälitystä" (Western Dollars Threaten News Transmission in Russia). *Helsingin Sanomat*, 13 May.

Zassoursky, Ivan. 1996. "Stanovlenie rossiskogo instituta SMI v kontekste globalnykh informatsionnykh protsessov" (Developing the Russian Mass Media in the Context of the Global Information Processes). Master's thesis, Department of the Foreign Journalism and Literature, Moscow State University.

———. 1999. *Mass-media vtoroi respubliki* (The Mass Media of the Second Republic). Moscow: Publishing House of the Moscow State University.

———. 2000. "The Rise and Transformation of the Media-Political System." Paper presented at the International Association for Media and Communication Research Conference in Singapore, 17–20 July.

———. Forthcoming. *The Mass Media in the Second Republic.*

Zassoursky, Yassen N. 1998. "Changing Media and Communications." In *Changing Media and Communications*, edited by Yassen N. Zassoursky and Elena Vartanova, 14–31. Moscow: Faculty of Journalism/Publisher IKAR.

———. 2000. "New Trends in Russian Media and Communications." Paper presented at the International Association for Media and Communication Research Conference in Singapore, 17–20 July.

Zassoursky, Yassen N., and Elena Vartanova. 1999a. "Transformation in the Context of Transition: Development of New Information and Communication Technologies within Professional Legal and Political Frameworks." In *Information Societies: Crises in the Making?*, 320–30. Montreal: Orbicom.

———. 1999b. "Transformation in the Context of Transition: Development of New Information and Communication Technologies in Five Eastern European Countries." Paper presented at the International Association for Media and Communication Research Conference in Leipzig, 27–31 July.

———. 2000. "Russian Television in Transition: Anything But Public." Paper presented at the 22d General Assembly and Scientific Conference in Singapore, July 17–20.

Zhilina, T. Yu. 1998. Interview by author. Moscow, July.

Index

About the Author

Terhi Rantanen is director of the MSc programme in Global Media and Communications at London School of Economics and Political Science. Previously, she held a full-time position in the Department of Communication at Helsinki University, where she also holds the position of Docent. She has also been a visiting fellow/scholar at several universities around the world including the UK, United States, Russia, and Australia.

Her research interests have focused on the global and national in international communications. Most of her research has been on news agencies, which provide excellent case studies for the study of globalization and the introduction of new communications technologies. One of the outcomes is a jointly written and edited (with Oliver Boyd-Barrett) book, *The Globalization of News*, published by Sage in 1998.